PRAYING
a Christ-Centered
ROSARY

PRAYING
a Christ-Centered
ROSARY
Meditations on the Mysteries

JAMES L. PAPANDREA

AVE MARIA PRESS AVE Notre Dame, Indiana

© 2021 by James L. Papandrea

All rights reserved. No part of this book may be used or reproduced in any manner whatsoever, except in the case of reprints in the context of reviews, without written permission from Ave Maria Press®, Inc., P.O. Box 428, Notre Dame, IN 46556, 1-800-282-1865.

Founded in 1865, Ave Maria Press is a ministry of the United States Province of Holy Cross.

www.avemariapress.com

Paperback: ISBN-13 978-1-59471-957-8

E-book: ISBN-13 978-1-59471-958-5

Cover image © World History Archive / Alamy Stock Photo.

Cover and text design by Christopher D. Tobin.

Printed and bound in the United States of America.

Library of Congress Cataloging-in-Publication Data
Names: Papandrea, James L., 1963- author.
Title: Praying a Christ-centered Rosary : meditations on the mysteries / James L. Papandrea.
Description: Notre Dame, Indiana : Ave Maria Press, 2021. | Includes bibliographical references. | Summary: "In this book, James L. Papandrea focuses on the mysteries beyond the Gospel events and taps into two millennia of theological reflection and connects each of the twenty mysteries of the Rosary to one of the deepest truths of Catholic faith in Christ"-- Provided by publisher.
Identifiers: LCCN 2020045219 | ISBN 9781594719578 (paperback) | ISBN 9781594719585 (ebook)
Subjects: LCSH: Mysteries of the Rosary--Meditations. | Jesus Christ--Biography--Meditations. | Prayer--Catholic Church--Meditations.
Classification: LCC BX2163 .P37 2021 | DDC 242/.74--dc23
LC record available at https://lccn.loc.gov/2020045219

Dedicated to the Memory of
Mae Vetrano
(1928–2019)

CONTENTS

INTRODUCTION
The Story of the Rosary

Praying with beads is an ancient tradition and has been a part of many religions, even before Christianity came along. But the Christian tradition of praying with beads actually started out with knots on a rope. Back in the early Middle Ages, monks were expected to pray all 150 psalms from the Bible every day. They used a rope with 150 knots on it to count off the psalms as they prayed. Monks who could not read (and people outside the monasteries who wanted to imitate the practice of the monks) were sometimes given permission to say the Our Father 150 times, instead of all the psalms. They used the knotted rope to count off 150 repetitions of the Lord's Prayer. At some point, beads replaced the knots, and the string of beads came to be called a "paternoster," for the first two words of the Our Father in Latin: *Pater noster.* At this time, a priest might prescribe the recitation of a Paternoster as a penance after Confession. Since 150 beads would make for a very long strand, the most common string of beads had a total of 50; the person praying would go around the string three times to reach the total of 150 prayers.

Later in the Middle Ages, collections of prayers circulated, including prayers asking for Mary's intercession. Inspired by the association of Mary with roses, a collection of prayers such as this would be called a "little rose garden," or *Rosarium* (hence the English word "rosary"). Some of the prayers to Mary were very ancient, such as the one known as Sub Tuum Praesidium (which we'll look at later). Others were responses from the Little Office of the Blessed Virgin. The prayer for Mary's intercession that became the most popular was the Ave Maria, or "Hail Mary."

Most of the Hail Mary prayer is taken directly from scripture. The first line, "Hail, Mary, full of grace, the Lord is with you," is quoted from the words of the archangel Gabriel as recorded in Luke 1:28. The only element that's added there is Mary's name. The angel addressed her directly, so he didn't say her name, but rather something similar to, "Hail, you who are full of grace . . ." So the prayer includes Mary's name for clarity. The second line of the prayer, "Blessed are you among women, and blessed is the fruit of your womb, Jesus," is quoted from the words of Mary's relative Elizabeth, as recorded in Luke 1:42. There again, the only word added is the name of Jesus, just as the name of Mary was added in the first line. The rest of the Hail Mary is simply a prayer for her intercession. We call her "Holy Mary" and "Mother of God," an ancient title that Christians have used for Mary since the early centuries of the Church. Then we ask her to "pray for us sinners, now and at the hour of our death."

No one knows exactly when the Hail Mary prayer was written, but it was already in use long before the turn of the thirteenth century, when St. Dominic promoted the praying of the Rosary. There is a tradition that St. Dominic invented the Rosary, but that's probably not true. He did encourage its use, as others did after him, but at this time the expectation was still that a person would pray the Our Father or the Hail Mary (or possibly just the first half of the Hail Mary) 150 times. Even then, however, the point was not simply repetition. These prayers were meant to facilitate meditation on the Incarnation and other events in the life of Christ, especially his Passion.

In the fourteenth century, the fifty beads were strung in groups of ten (called decades) with a larger, offset bead in between. The ten beads were for the Hail Mary, and the single bead was for the Our Father. As people were still going around three times, that totaled fifteen decades. The Joyful, Sorrowful, and Glorious

Mysteries were meditated upon every time one prayed the Rosary; they were not divided by days of the week as they are now. (The Luminous Mysteries were added by Pope St. John Paul II in 2002.) In 1569, Pope Pius V gave the Rosary official endorsement with the encyclical *Consueverunt Romani*.

Many miracles have been associated with Mary's intercession, and we'll highlight some of them in this book. Of particular note is the 1571 Battle of Lepanto. As Muslim Turkish invaders from the Ottoman Empire threatened to take over Europe, the fate of the West came down to one decisive battle in the Gulf of Lepanto, the gateway to the Adriatic Sea and Western Europe. Pope Pius V called for all Catholics to pray the Rosary for victory, and although the Christian forces were outnumbered, they prevailed. Even though the Holy League's navy had fewer ships, they had superior canons and favorable winds, and the Christian slaves rowing the Turkish ships rebelled against their masters. The battle was won on October 7, and Europe was kept safe.

In 1572, the pope declared October 7 the Feast of Mary, Queen of Victory, and later also the Feast of Mary, Queen of the Most Holy Rosary. From this, and numerous other cases of divine intervention, Mary's intercession has proven a strong help for those who are devoted to her Son and who pray her Rosary. But it should be noted that even when the feast day was declared, the Rosary still did not have the exact form it has today. Christians have always prayed the Rosary in a variety of ways, with variation in prayers. There is no single correct way to pray the Rosary.

Praying When It's Hard to Pray

Praying an ancient or traditional prayer is one way that we can pray, even when we don't know what to pray for. Have you ever felt so overwhelmed that words failed you? And have you ever felt that words failed you at exactly the time when you most wished you could express your helplessness and frustration to your heavenly Father? Perhaps you have been comforted by these words from the apostle Paul: "The Spirit also comes to the aid of our weakness; for we do not know how to pray as we ought, but the Spirit [himself] intercedes with inexpressible groanings. And the one who searches hearts knows what is the intention of the Spirit, because [the Spirit] intercedes for the holy ones according to God's will" (Rom 8:26–27). The prayers used in the Rosary offer one way that we can pray without having to think about the words, simply letting the Holy Spirit pray for us in our need, and asking Mother Mary to intercede on our behalf. The Holy Spirit is called our Advocate in the gospels, and Mary is also called our advocate in the prayer that begins "Hail Holy Queen" (Salve Regina).

Mary Points to Jesus

Perhaps most important is the fact that everything we know about Mary, and everything we believe about Mary, points us to her Son, Jesus. Even the specific doctrines surrounding the life of Mary, such as her Immaculate Conception and her assumption, are related to what we believe about Jesus Christ and teach us something about him. As we will see when we explore the various mysteries in the chapters that follow, the lives of Mary and Jesus are intertwined. Mary gave Jesus to the world, and Jesus gave Mary to the Church (see John 19:27).

Just as we read in the account of the Wedding at Cana (Jn 2:1–11), Mary's intercession has some influence over her Son. But as we see in that account, her role in the Church is always to give us a perfect example of accepting the will of God, and as she said to the stewards at the wedding, she says to the Church: "Do whatever he tells you."

Something to Think About

On a personal note, I did not grow up praying the Rosary. Although I was baptized in the Catholic Church, I was raised in a Protestant denomination. I found my way back to the Church after getting my PhD in the study of early Christianity. But even after coming back into the Catholic Church, I didn't see myself "getting into the Rosary" for a long time.

It's not that I resisted it or had any objection to it; it's just that I didn't think it was for me. My faith was mostly in my head, and heavily dependent on words, and I was slow to appreciate the value of ancient and traditional prayers in my own devotional life. Add to that the fact that I'm not good at multitasking; at first I found it difficult to pray the words of the Hail Mary while at the same time meditating on the mysteries. In fact, I found it hard to think about what I should think about.

In any case, if you're like me, I hope this book will help you learn to meditate on the mysteries. Each of the twenty mysteries will be presented as paradoxes—that is, deep and wonderful truths that would seem to be contradictions if not for faith. These paradoxes are to be embraced more than explained (although I will do some explaining) so that, as St. Bonaventure said, the mystery of the paradoxes will inspire us to awe and reverence. In one sense, when we meditate on the mysteries of the Rosary we are celebrating and giving thanks to God for the times when the heavenly realm breaks through into our world. In the process, we are reminded that God is always at work—in our lives, and everywhere around us.

Both Heart and Head

Some people think of the Rosary as an elementary kind of devotion, perhaps boring or even beneath them, as though it's for spiritual beginners. If that's you (and it used to be me), I would encourage you to consider that maybe you've been trying too hard to put everything into words. It might be good to get back to something simpler, at least as one part of your devotional life.

Take my word for it: praying the Rosary can actually draw you deeper into meditation than you ever thought possible.

Most religions recognize the value of meditation. Buddhists, Hindus, and Taoists all have their forms of meditation. We have the Rosary. It is our specifically Catholic form of meditation. In it we are not emptying our minds, focusing on ourselves, or reaching out into the void—we are connecting with the Creator of the universe, and asking his Mother to intercede with him on our behalf.

Some people love the Rosary but grow impatient with theological reflection, as though it is overly intellectual—and maybe even pointless, since it's all a mystery anyway. If that's you, I encourage you to open your mind to the deep well of theological mystery inherent in the Rosary. I promise it's not hard to understand, unless you overthink it and try to grasp it completely. If you let go of the idea of mastering the mystery, and instead submit to it, praying the Rosary will enrich your devotional life and enliven your faith with new insights. Treat these insights into the mysteries as ways of visualizing the events they recall; see the life of Jesus through the eyes of Mary.

I've found that imagining a scene or picture helps keep the mystery in my mind as I pray along the beads, and the mystery itself becomes a visual backdrop for the prayers—setting the scene, if you will. It's much like the way many Christians use icons in their devotional lives, or follow artistic depictions of the Way of the Cross as they pray the Stations. In fact, a picture or an icon can be extremely helpful as a summary of what we're meditating on. A picture really is worth a thousand words, and a visual image of one of the mysteries of the Rosary can instantly encapsulate and help you retain the words that might describe and explain the mystery, in a deep and meaningful way.

I encourage you to take time to look up artistic depictions and icons of the events of the mysteries. Many great artists have given us beautiful paintings and other works of art that can help us visualize the mysteries while we meditate on them. Sometimes, that visualization does most of the work of meditation for us! If you go online and view the ways that great artists have depicted the mysteries over the centuries, put together a digital folder of your favorites, ones you can go back to again and again. Or better yet, print them or buy framed versions, and hang them in your home.

This book is an attempt to bring together the head and the heart in the beautiful devotion of the Rosary, focusing on Jesus Christ, through his Mother, Mary. You might read through this book at one time, and then keep its reflections in mind as a background to your meditations on the mysteries. Or you might keep the book handy as you pray the Rosary, reading parts of it to serve as your meditations. You might even go back and forth. Rosary groups may find that reading relevant sections before praying each decade will deepen their meditation on Christ. And you may find the same.

However you choose to use this book, you will be rewarded if you take it slowly and open your mind and heart to the depths of these mysteries, giving gratitude to the Blessed Trinity for the Incarnation.

PART 1

The Joyful Mysteries (Mondays and Saturdays)

A Mystery in History: Fatima and the Miracle of the Sun

In May of 1917, the Mother of God appeared to three young children in Fatima, Portugal. At the time, Jacinta, Francisco, and Lucia were seven, eight, and ten years old, respectively. After praying the Rosary with the innocent, childlike faith that Jesus praised (Mt 18:3), Mother Mary appeared to them and referred to herself as Our Lady of the Rosary. She would appear to them five more times, encouraging them to pray the Rosary for an end to World War I. But when the people of their village heard about what they had seen, the adults doubted and scoffed. So the Blessed Mother promised a miracle that would convince the people that the children were telling the truth.

On October 13, 1917, more than 70,000 people showed up to see if there was really going to be a miracle. They were not disappointed. The sun moved in the sky, changed colors, and then seemed to move closer to earth. The rain-soaked ground was immediately dried. Eyewitnesses said the sun was easy to look at without squinting, and some said they saw an image of the Virgin Mary. The whole crowd fell to its knees; many eyes filled up with tears. Numerous sick or infirmed people were healed, and many skeptics were convinced.

It is interesting to notice that in the book of Revelation, Mary is described as the woman "clothed with the sun" (Rv 12:1). In 1930, the Church confirmed that the events that occurred in Fatima were, in fact, a miracle, and Francisco and Jacinta have since been canonized as saints. There is much more to this visitation of the Blessed Virgin Mary to the children of Fatima, but for us it's important to emphasize that Mary encouraged us to pray the Rosary daily and affirmed its power.

1.

THE ANNUNCIATION

The Paradox of a Virgin Mother

What is the Annunciation?

Read Luke 1:26–38.

The word *annunciation* simply means to announce something. In this case, it's the announcement of the most important event in history: the long-awaited coming of the Messiah. As we read in John's gospel, this is when "the Word became flesh and made his dwelling among us" (Jn 1:14). This is what we call the *Incarnation*, that is, the *embodiment* of the divine and eternal Word, when God the Son acquired a human nature and came to live a life that was fully human. Maybe you haven't thought about it in this way before, but the moment when "the Word became flesh" was not the time of his birth in the stable of Bethlehem. It was the moment of his conception. And that moment is captured for us in the first chapter of Luke's gospel.

The archangel Gabriel came to Mary and announced to her God's plan for the redemption of the world (the angel's three visits to Joseph are recorded in Matthew's gospel, chapters 1 and 2). This was God's plan to make salvation possible for all people. And that plan included Mary, if she was willing. It would be *in* her that divinity would unite with humanity; it would be *from* her that divinity would receive a human body; and it would be *through* her that divinity would enter into space and time to become one of us, and to be with us. This is the single most important event in human history. And it happened, near as we can tell, in about the year 5 BC.

But wait—doesn't BC stand for "before Christ"? If he was born in 5 BC, how could he be born five years before himself? The answer to that is complicated, but it has to do with the fact that the system of dating years that we use now is actually off by four to six years. The ones who created this calendar did so long after "the year of the Lord" (the English translation of *Anno Domini*, or AD), and so although they did their best to try to count back to Jesus' birth, they missed the mark. But Luke was not off the mark; he knew his dates, and he tells us that Gabriel came to Mary with this announcement, "in the days of Herod, King of Judea" (Lk 1:5). This is Herod I, and he died in what we would call by our calendars 4 BC. So Mary conceived Jesus no later than 4 BC, and when you factor in the other events that happened after Jesus' birth while Herod was still alive, it seems reasonable that Jesus Christ was conceived, and then born, in the year 5 BC. According to the Western tradition, the annunciation took place on March 25, and the birth of Jesus took place exactly nine months later, on December 25.

In the Nicene Creed, we say that Christ "came down from heaven." This line may seem like a no-brainer, but it's very important. In the history of the Church, there have been those who have wanted to argue that Jesus Christ was not the Word made flesh but really just a mere human who earned God's favor through obedience. This is a heresy called adoptionism, because it is speculated that God adopted Jesus as his Son at his Baptism, which means Jesus was not the Only Begotten Son who shared the divine nature with the Father and the Holy Spirit. To be clear, that idea is a heresy. The words "came down" (along with that fun word *consubstantial*) were put into the Creed to emphasize that Jesus Christ is not someone who started out as a mere human and elevated himself.

Actually, he is the opposite: he started out as God and humbled himself to descend to us and become one of us.

Not only that, but he was willing to veil his glory, and temporarily limit his omnipotence, omniscience, and omnipresence to be truly human. After all, he could not experience the weaknesses and vulnerabilities of the human condition and still be all-powerful, all-knowing, and everywhere at once. He did not lose or give up these divine attributes (because he did not become any less divine). Nevertheless, he was willing to "empty himself" (Phil 2:6–7), meaning voluntarily limit himself, or in a way, set aside these divine powers, so that he could grow, learn, suffer, and die "for us men and for our salvation" (see also Luke 2:52). Have you ever heard that rhetorical question, "Can God make a rock so big that even he himself can't lift it?" The answer is he did—not by making the rock bigger but by making himself smaller. You see he was so almighty, so all-powerful, that he even had the power to limit himself. Of course, it was only the Son who limited himself and became incarnate, not the Father or the Holy Spirit.

To be perfectly clear, the annunciation was not simply the announcement of God's intervention—it was also the *start* of it. The angel did not tell Mary something that would happen later. He was telling her what was going to happen that day, assuming she agreed. Of course, she did agree to it, and our Lord was conceived in her womb immediately. And it should go without saying that if the human life of Jesus Christ began at his conception, that means that all human life begins at conception. To say otherwise is to deny the meaning of the annunciation and question the Incarnation.

Where was Mary?

As we think about these meditations on the mysteries, let's consider each scene and try to see it through the eyes of Mary. If we can imagine where she was, what she saw, and whom she encountered, this can become a visual backdrop for our meditation when we are praying the Rosary.

It was six months after Mary's relative Elizabeth had conceived John (so we know Jesus was six months younger than his cousin the baptizer). Mary was in her hometown of Nazareth, in Galilee. Most of the paintings of this scene, such as my personal favorite from Renaissance painter Sandro Botticelli, show Mary sitting alone, reading the scriptures. We know from tradition that she was a very faithful Jewish girl who had been dedicated to God by her parents, though we don't know if she was really reading the scriptures when the archangel showed up.

When the archangel appeared, he greeted Mary with what has become the first line of our Hail Mary prayer: "Hail [Mary], full of grace, the Lord is with you . . ." Mary's name was added for clarity and emphasis, and so that it could become a prayer for us. But Gabriel actually just called her "full of grace." This meant that she was unique among all of humanity (not counting her Son), in the sense that she was, what my Wesleyan friends would call, entirely sanctified. She was (and is) perfectly pure, and fully formed as a woman of God; she had "come to share in the divine nature" (2 Pt 1:4). She was the only mere human ever to be in a state of perfect grace since the fall.

Since Mary was uniquely pure, she was not burdened with the effects of the fall of humanity (we'll talk about this later) and so she had no original sin to hinder her free will. We all have free will, but Mary's will was truly and fully free, freer than the rest of ours. This is important because Mary's participation in God's plan had to be voluntary. God was not going to force Mary to play her part. She had to accept it freely, and she did. After asking a couple of questions, she was ready to say, "May it be done to me according to your word."

The Latin word that is translated "May it be done" is *fiat*. If you've ever heard about Mary's *fiat*, that's what this was. It was her moment of submitting her own will to the will of God, and it is in this that she became the perfect example for us to follow. Her own Son, Jesus, would follow in her footsteps by submitting his human will to the divine will in the Garden of Gethsemane. But the point to think about now is that Mary is the first person of the new covenant who truly and willingly cooperated with God to bring about salvation. We can each do this on a small scale. It's called *synergy*, "working together" with God for our own salvation, as St. Paul said: "Work out your own salvation with fear and trembling; for it is God who is at work in you, enabling you both to will and to work for his good pleasure" (Phil 2:12–13, NRSV).

By saying "yes" to God's plan for salvation, Mary reversed what Eve did in the Garden of Eden when she said "no" to God and disobeyed. In fact, many writers throughout the history of the Church have pointed out that the Latin version of Eve—*Eva*—when reversed spells *Ave*, the Latin word that begins the Hail Mary. Eve was tempted by a fallen angel, but Mary was greeted with reverence and humility by an archangel. And although death came into the world through Eve, life came into the world through Mary. As St. Irenaeus wrote in the late second century, Mary untied the knot that was tied by Eve, so that through Mary even Eve might be saved.

What does it tell us about Jesus?

The concept of a Virgin Mother is a paradox; it seems like a contradiction, and it can only be accepted by faith. In this case, the paradox is also a miracle. Jesus' conception was a direct work of God, suspending the usual laws of nature as we perceive them and breaking through into the world of time and three-dimensional space. And the result is that Mary had the unique dual vocation of virginal celibacy and married motherhood.

Mary was a virgin when she conceived, and she remained a virgin even after the birth of Jesus. In fact, she remained a virgin all her life. We call this her *perpetual virginity*. Sometimes she is referred to as Mary, *Ever-Virgin*. She is the eternal Virgin Mother of Christ. But to be clear, she really did give birth to a real flesh-and-blood baby. Although there was some speculation in the early Church that maybe Jesus came out of her like a beam of light, the Church Fathers agreed that she did really give birth (though they could not agree on whether she felt the pain of childbirth, based on Genesis 3:16, but see Revelation 12:2). Nevertheless, even though she gave birth as every mother does, she remained a virgin. How is this possible? St. Jerome said it was possible in the same way that the resurrected Jesus could enter a room when the door was locked. It was a miracle.

The important point is that Jesus was Mary's only child. It's true that the New Testament mentions some "brothers" of the Lord (and two of these even wrote the letters of James and Jude), but the word for "brothers" here has a broad meaning, and would include any relatives of the same generation, such as cousins. The proof that Mary had no other children is that Jesus, speaking from the Cross, entrusts her to John—which he would never have done (or legally been able to do) if she had other children. Mary was able to be completely devoted to her one and only Son, Jesus, and in this, she is once again a perfect example for us to follow.

As *Ever-Virgin*, Mary is ageless. You hardly ever see paintings of an old Mary. This has as much to do with her incorruptibility (another topic we'll get to later) as her perpetual virginity. But according to the early Church tradition, she lived to be around eighty-five years old. To be clear, neither our salvation nor even Mary's assumption and coronation depend on her remaining celibate. None of that would have been ruined if she had had other children after Jesus, because that's not a sin; it's just as much a simple historical fact as anything symbolic or with deeper meaning. The point is Mary's own dedication to God (beginning with her parents dedicating her) is parallel to Jesus' dedication to God, beginning when she presented him to God in the Temple.

Whenever we see in scripture a story about an older or apparently barren couple conceiving a child, the point there is that this is God doing something. It's not left up to chance or nature, and it's not accomplished by human strength or ingenuity. It is a work of God; it is a miracle. So if that's the case for those biblical babies who have two parents, how much more is it the case for Jesus, who was conceived not by a human man but by the Holy Spirit? The Holy Spirit is the immanent (up close and personal) presence of God. This is the same Holy Spirit who hovered over the void at creation, the same Holy Spirit who hovered over the tent of the presence of God in the desert, the same Holy Spirit who hovered over the tabernacle in the Temple; this is the Holy Spirit who hovered over the Virgin, resulting in the conception of Jesus Christ, and the same Holy Spirit who comes down to hover over the altar to turn the bread and wine into the Body and Blood of Christ. The fact that Jesus' conception is a miracle, the paradox of the Virgin Mother, shows that God had taken the reins, and was intervening to do something decisive.

But we should be careful here. When John's gospel tells us that the Word *became* flesh, it does not mean that divinity changed into humanity (in the way that the bread and wine change into the Body and Blood). In fact, it doesn't mean that divinity changed at all. Divinity was united to humanity in the person of Jesus Christ, but in his incarnation he did not become any less divine. He started out fully divine, and remains eternally fully divine. He acquired a real human nature at his conception, and from that moment in history, he remains eternally fully human.

The presence of God was with the Ark of the Covenant in the Old Testament story of the Exodus, and the Ark held the words of God on the tablets of Moses. Similarly, Mary is the Ark of the New Covenant, because the presence of God was with her, and her womb held the Word of God, Jesus Christ.

Perhaps one point of all this is to emphasize what should be obvious: that in the coming of Jesus Christ, God was intervening in human history. The coming of Christ *is* divine intervention, and is the most important event in history.

What aspects of this mystery should we imitate?

In the annunciation, God invited Mary to have an important role in the salvation of humanity. But Mary had a choice. And when she said "yes" to God's will and God's plan, she became the perfect saintly example of those who do God's will and cooperate with his work in the world. To imitate this mystery is to say "yes" to God.

MEDITATION

Mary is the Virgin Mother, who remains a virgin as a mother. She is the Untier of Knots and the Ark of the New Covenant. God prepared Mary to be the mother of his Son long before she conceived him in her womb.

2.

THE VISITATION
The Paradox of the Mother of God

What is the Visitation?

Read Luke 1:39–56.

The Visitation is the trip that Mary made to see her relative Elizabeth, who had conceived John the baptizer with God's help (and in this case, with her husband's help) six months before Jesus was conceived. Luke tells us that Mary left to visit Elizabeth after the annunciation and stayed about three months. So it's safe to assume that Mary intended to be there for the birth of John, probably to help.

When Mary arrived, it seems that the two babies sensed each other's presence; when Elizabeth heard the sound of Mary's voice, her baby "leaped" in her womb. Then Luke tells us she was filled with the Holy Spirit. Some of the early Church Fathers believed that John was filled with the Holy Spirit first, and that his "leap" in Elizabeth's womb was his first act of prophecy, having been filled with joy at the coming of the Savior. So he was announcing the coming of the Messiah before he was even born! (Again, this is evidence that the baby in the womb is a person, and some Church Fathers connected the Visitation to Psalm 139, "For it was you who formed my inward parts; you knit me together in my mother's womb" v. 13, NRSV.)

But Elizabeth, too, was filled with the Holy Spirit, and also prophesied. She knew that the baby in Mary's womb was the Savior of the world, and so therefore Mary is "the Mother of the Lord."

Then Elizabeth exclaims what eventually became the second line of our Hail Mary prayer: "Blessed are you among women and blessed is the fruit of your womb [Jesus]." Again, the prayer adds the name of Jesus for clarity and emphasis, but other than that, the first half of the Hail Mary is right out of scripture—straight from the mouths of an archangel and St. Elizabeth.

Immediately after the women exchange greetings, Mary, too, speaks prophetically. As she sings the Magnificat, she predicts that all generations will call her blessed, which is what we do whenever we pray the Rosary. Both mothers and both babies were filled with the Holy Spirit that day (Jesus was in a unique and permanent way, of course). This reminds us that the Holy Spirit fills both men and women, and that both men and women (and even children) can be proclaimers of the Good News of the Savior.

Where was Mary?

Luke tells us that Elizabeth lived in "a Judean town in the hill country." I don't know of any ancient tradition that tells us exactly which town this was. Today, pilgrims to the Holy Land often visit the Church of the Visitation in Ein Karem, but several towns have been suggested as possibilities, including Hebron, which is more than 100 miles from Nazareth. It probably would have taken Mary at least a week to travel there, and it would have been a difficult journey into a hard country. But if you think about it, Mary was going to be with the only other woman she knew of who might believe her story, and be able to relate to it.

Remember, the story of an aged woman conceiving emphasizes that it was God's action, though in Elizabeth's case she did conceive by her husband. Hers was not a virginal conception, but it was still a miraculous one. In fact, as we will see later, John's miraculous birth was a lot like Mary's own, as her parents (Sts. Joachim and Anna) had a story similar to that of Zechariah and Elizabeth.

You can imagine young Mary coming into a secluded hill town that rarely received visitors. Maybe she was riding on a donkey (though it seems that might be difficult for a pregnant woman), or perhaps she was riding in a cart pulled by a donkey. Some people believe St. Joseph went with her on this trip; others say he did not. As she entered the small village, some of the townspeople might have stared at her, wondering who she was. Others might have greeted her. She would ask where Elizabeth was, and she would probably find her working, despite being more than six months pregnant. The two relatives would have a tearful reunion, and eventually find some time to be alone together so that they could compare notes. Then they would marvel at the works of God that had affected them so directly, and how God would use two small-town women to fulfill his plan for the salvation of humanity.

Elizabeth's words, that Mary is "the Mother of my Lord," anticipate one of the Church's most important titles for Mary. Since Mary is not the mother of Jesus' humanity only but also the mother of his whole personhood—including his divine nature— she is called the Mother of God. So the mystery of the Visitation is for us the paradox of the Mother of God. How can God have a mother? Well, when we say that Mary is the Mother of God, we are not saying that she's the mother of God the Father. And we're not saying that she's the mother of God the Spirit. We're not saying anything about Divinity being born or having a beginning. But we are saying that the divinity of Christ came into the world through Mary: she carried Divinity in her womb, and she delivered Divinity into the world.

What does it tell us about Jesus?

Perhaps the greatest mystery of all the mysteries is how the divine nature of Jesus could remain fully divine and also be contained within a woman's womb. This is the real heart of the Mother of

God paradox. That's because one attribute of divinity is omnipresence, which means that God is everywhere at once, in all times and places, and cannot be contained by anything. God is above and apart from creation, not contained within it.

The theological term for this is that God is *uncircumscribable*. To *circumscribe* literally means to "draw around something," but in this sense it means to contain something. So to say that God is *uncircumscribable* means that God is "uncontainable," that God cannot be contained by anything. And yet the divine nature of Jesus (which is the same divinity as the Father and the Spirit) *was contained* within the womb of Mary. Omnipresence circumscribed. For me, this is the greatest paradox, the deepest mystery, the most wonderful wonder of all. The Creator didn't just acquire a human nature; he accepted the limitations of the human body. He didn't just become human; he became a human fetus. And the woman who carried and delivered him is the Mother of God.

If you ever go to a Greek church, you might hear the word *Theotokos*. This is the Greek word that means "Mother of God," or more literally, the "God-bearer." Theotokos has been an important title for Mary since at least the third century. In the fifth century, there was a controversy in the eastern part of the Church over whether we really should call Mary the Mother of God. Some people worried that it would be misunderstood, including the archbishop of Constantinople—a guy by the name of Nestorius, who would eventually be declared a heretic. Finally a council was held in the year 431, in the city of Ephesus. This came to be called the Third Ecumenical Council, and one of its most important decisions was to confirm the existing tradition of calling Mary the Mother of God.

All of our Marian doctrines tell us as much or more about Jesus than they do about Mary. In this case, the affirmation of the title Mother of God is also an affirmation of Jesus' divinity and of the inseparable union of that divinity with his humanity. He is not two persons, one divine and one human; he is one Person, who exists forever in two natures, divine and human. This is important for us because it is the union of humanity with divinity in Jesus Christ that makes *our* union with God possible. By uniting humanity with divinity in his incarnation, the Son of God set the precedent for our humanity to be united with God—that is, reconciled to our Creator. So the one whom the whole world could not contain was contained in Mary's womb. And this shows us God's love for us and willingness to unite with our humanity, to heal it, and to save it. This is why we call Mary the Mother of God.

We know that St. Joseph didn't participate in the conception of Jesus. That means Jesus got his human DNA from Mary. The Church Fathers often said that he was the Son of God in his divinity, and the Son of Mary in his humanity. But Mary also got something from him. Mothers know that there is a biological bond that a mother shares with her child that never goes away. For Mary, I believe that her biological bond with Jesus completed her own Immaculate Conception, solidified her incorruptibility, and ensured her assumption and coronation (concepts we will explore later). Mary had a bond with Jesus (and with his divinity) that no one else could ever have, because she held his divinity inside her. So when St. Paul says that "in him dwells the whole fullness of the deity bodily" (Col 2:9), it is also true that the fullness of deity dwelt in the body of Mary too, for nine months. And so if Jesus is the Prince of the kingdom of God, then Mary is the Queen Mother.

Jesus is the Son of God by nature: he shares the same divine nature with the Father and the Spirit. But we are also sons and daughters of God, not by nature but by adoption. John tells us that "to those who did accept him he gave power to become children of God, to those who believe in his name" (Jn 1:12). So we become children of God the Father; he is our Father, as he is Jesus'

Father (cf. Jn 20:17). That means we are Jesus' adopted brothers and sisters, and Mary is also our Mother. Another title for Mary is Mother of the Church, because we are "the rest of her children" (Rv 12:17, NRSV). John understood all of this because when Jesus spoke some of his last words from the Cross, he said to Mary (referring to John), "Woman, behold your son," and he said to John (referring to Mary), "Behold, your mother" (Jn 19:26–27). At that moment John stood in for all of us, for the Church, as the adopted son of Mary. She is our Mother, too.

Paintings of Mary and the infant Jesus, and especially icons of the *Theotokos*, often depict Jesus on Mary's lap. That makes sense, but it's also deeply theological. Mary is the Seat of Wisdom, and Wisdom himself sits on her lap; and of course when he's on her lap, he is also right in front of her womb. The Word and the Wisdom of God took on human life inside Mary, and was given to the world through her. At the beginning of his life he is centered in her, and in the end he will share his heavenly throne with her.

What aspects of this mystery should we imitate?

Elizabeth recognized Mary as the Mother of God. To give reverence to Mary, to be devoted to her, to pray to her and ask for her intercession, is to recognize the fragile human fetus in her womb for who he is. Only then can we appreciate Mary for who she is and receive the blessings of her motherhood.

MEDITATION

Mary is the Mother of God, who contained the uncontainable Word of God in her womb. She is the Seat of Wisdom and the Mother of the Church.

3.

THE NATIVITY
The Paradox of the Helpless King

What is the Nativity?

Read Luke 2:1–20 and Matthew 1:18–2:12.

The Nativity is, of course, the birth of Christ. It's what we celebrate at Christmas, and so for this mystery, you can think about all the things that come to mind when you think of Christmas. Traveling (Mary did that), worrying about where to stay (Mary did that), planning the logistics of meals (Mary did that), and receiving gifts (Mary did that). Mary did many of the same things we do at Christmastime, but without the relaxation of time off work, and without the comforts of a warm bed or a roaring fire. And her midnight Mass was giving birth to Jesus. The straw was the altar on which she laid the body of the Lord, who ironically was probably crying like the babies in the back of the church who perhaps would rather be in bed at midnight on Christmas Eve. Some of the Church Fathers noted that the manger foreshadows the eucharistic table. Jesus is placed where animals' food goes, and later he will be our spiritual food on the altar.

The story of that first Christmas is told in Luke and Matthew, but neither one has the whole story. Luke includes the shepherds, and Matthew has the Magi (M for Matthew & M for Magi; that's how I always remember it). Matthew assures us that the birth of Jesus is the fulfillment of a promise: "The virgin shall be with child and bear a son, and they shall name him Emmanuel, which means, 'God is with us'" (cf. Is 7:14). And so the Word became flesh, and this shivering baby was (and is) "God with us."

Where was Mary?

It may seem like Palestine two thousand years ago was a pretty backward place for God to come into the world. Sure, they didn't have the modern conveniences we take for granted. But they did have a common language that most everyone in the Roman world could speak: Greek. And there was a certain amount of peace around the empire that made travel possible, if not safe. Yes, you could argue that peace at the point of a spear is not the same thing as freedom, but it did allow for news to travel quickly, especially the Good News. So it turns out that Jesus came at the perfect time: the only time before now when there was a "world language," and one of the few times in history without war in the Middle East. Never before or since was the world in such a position to be ready to receive its Savior. The timing was perfect, because it was God's timing.

When Herod asked around to try to figure out where Jesus was born, the prophet Micah was consulted. He had written, "And you, Bethlehem, land of Judah, are by no means least among the rulers of Judah; since from you shall come a ruler, who is to shepherd my people Israel" (cf. Micah 5:1–2). And so, Mary had to travel again. Just as she had traveled to see Elizabeth when she was newly pregnant, and traveled home again when she was three or four months along, now she was going to have to travel when she was more than eight months pregnant.

The trip to Bethlehem is not quite as far as Elizabeth's village probably was, but it would still have taken the better part of a week for Joseph and Mary to make the journey. It would have been an expensive trip. Meals along the way. Tolls. And don't forget: the whole point of the trip was that they had to pay a tax. The expense must have added stress to an already difficult journey.

When they got to Bethlehem, the inn was full. Before I began studying scripture, I used to imagine Joseph and Mary going from inn to inn, knocking on the doors, and being turned away at each one, growing more and more disappointed and desperate with each closing door—as if some big convention was in town and all the hotel rooms were booked up. But if you read the scripture carefully, it says, "There was no place for them in the inn." The inn. Singular. There was only one inn, because Bethlehem was a pretty small town. There was no place for Joseph and Mary to stay, so they did the only thing they could: they stayed in a cave that was used for sheltering animals. Nowadays it gets down to about fifty degrees at night in Bethlehem in the winter. So there they are, in a cave, with animals. They can't start a fire because of all the hay. So they wrap up and snuggle in for the night. But then . . . well, God's timing is God's timing. In the Western Church we celebrate Jesus' birth on December 25 because that is exactly nine months after the annunciation on March 25, when Jesus was conceived. And so Jesus came into the world, Mary swaddled him tightly, and held him close.

But there was to be no peace and quiet for the Holy Family. Angels announced the birth of the Lord to the nearby shepherds, who came running to see. It seems they were still in the cave when the shepherds got there. Eventually the Holy Family was able to move into the inn, or maybe into the house of a compassionate Bethlehemite. And it was there that the Magi eventually found them. Then, just when Mary must have been thinking that it couldn't get any more chaotic, Gabriel came to Joseph in a dream and told him they had to be on the move again. King Herod was out to kill Jesus, so they fled to Egypt (Mt 2:13–23). The Lamb on the lam. Once again, homeless. St. Ambrose wrote that Jesus accepted homelessness so that we could go to his Father's home in heaven.

What does it tell us about Jesus?

The Nativity is another reminder of just how much God loves us, and just how much God is willing to do to call us to himself. The Word of God, who is God, and who shares the same divine nature with the Father and the Spirit, is omnipotent (all-powerful). But the omnipotent Word was willing to limit his power, accepting weakness and frailty, in order to become truly human and experience life as we know it. Without giving up or diminishing his divinity and his power as Creator of the universe, he was willing to be vulnerable enough to submit himself to the elements of nature, and even to the dangers of human greed and jealousy. And also to wear a diaper.

So the Nativity of Our Lord is the paradox of the helpless King, the almighty One who chose to be weak for our sake. St. Jerome said that he was born among beasts of burden because he would later carry the Cross and bear the burden of our sins. St. Gregory of Nazianzus wrote that he was wrapped in swaddling cloths, but later he would leave his burial cloths lying in the empty tomb.

Luke calls Jesus Mary's "firstborn Son" (2:7), not that she had other children after him, but that as the "firstborn" and a son, he was the one who would be dedicated to God according to Jewish law. He is the heir. We also call him the Only Begotten Son of God. That term, "Only Begotten," means that he is unique; he is the only one of his kind. No other human has ever been, or will ever be, like him, because he is fully divine as well as fully human. The fact that he is "begotten" refers to the divine nature that he gets from the Father, and shares with the Father and the Spirit. He is the Son of God by nature, and so he is the heir to all that is the

Father's, including eternal life in the kingdom. And now he shares his inheritance with us, his adopted brothers and sisters—we who are Mary's other children.

What aspects of this mystery should we imitate?

Love is always a risk. When we love, we take the risk that our love will be rejected. We make ourselves vulnerable to the will of others. That's what the divine Son of God did when he reached out in love to us, which he did by becoming a helpless baby. As John tells us, "He was in the world, and the world came to be through him, but the world did not know him. He came to what was his own, but his own people did not accept him" (Jn 1:10–11). But love is worth the risk. To imitate this mystery is to risk the inconvenience, the awkwardness, and the possible rejection of loving our neighbor in the name of Jesus. Love is a risk. We must take the risk.

MEDITATION

Jesus was the Creator who was willing to take the risk to subject himself to creation. He was the all-powerful One who was willing to limit his power and become vulnerable. He accepted the frailty of the human condition in order to allow us to transcend it.

4.

THE PRESENTATION
The Paradox of the Humble God

What is the Presentation?

Read Luke 2:22–40.

After returning from Egypt, Joseph and Mary brought Jesus to the holy Temple in Jerusalem. Since he was the "firstborn son," Hebrew law required that he be dedicated to the Lord, and Luke tells us that Mary brought her Son to the Temple to fulfill the law. The presentation required a sacrifice. But the Holy Family could not afford the usual animal sacrifice, so they were allowed to offer a pair of turtledoves or pigeons. This was a concession made for very poor people who could not afford to buy a four-footed animal for the sacrifice. It's nice to think of them offering doves, because the dove is a symbol for peace, and for the Holy Spirit.

But what happened to all the gold (not to mention the frankincense and myrrh)? I think we have to assume that the gifts of the Magi financed the sojourn in Egypt, and it had all been spent. When the Holy Family started that trip they might have been homeless, but at least they had some money. Now they had next to nothing. Again this reminds us that the King of Kings and Lord of Lords was not born into a palace, or to a wealthy family with money and connections. He was willing to be born into a humble situation. Born in a cave, running from the authorities, living out of a suitcase (or donkey sacks?), wandering in a foreign land among strangers, and then finally coming into the Temple with the minimal acceptable offering. He came into the world with cattle, was dedicated to God with doves, and rode to his last days on a donkey. This is humility incarnate.

But in the Temple there were two very faithful, and elderly, prophets, named Simeon and Anna. They recognized Jesus as the fulfillment of Israel's hopes, and they blessed the Holy Family, saying that this little boy was the answer to their prayers—and not theirs only but also the prayers of the whole people of God.

Where was Mary?

Jerusalem would have been a very chaotic place, exactly the kind of place that a young mother might want to keep her child away from. But Mary had been on the road so long it didn't matter at this point. She trusted God, so she knew that no harm would come to her Son. Still, it must have seemed strange to Mary that this old man whom she had never met wanted to hold her Son. According to the account in Luke's gospel, it doesn't even say that Simeon *asked* to hold Jesus. He just "took him in his arms" and started prophesying. And his words must have been even more disturbing to young Mary. He said, "Behold, this child is destined for the fall and the rise of many in Israel, and to be a sign that will be contradicted (and you yourself a sword will pierce) so that the thoughts of many hearts may be revealed."

Luke tells us that Simeon was filled with the Holy Spirit. And since we know the end of the story, we know what Simeon was talking about. The "sign that will be contradicted," or opposed, is the Cross (Jesus himself said he would be the cause of division among people; see Matthew 10:34–36). And Jesus' death on the Cross would break Mary's heart. We don't really know how much Mary knew about what was going to happen at this point. We don't know if Mary knew that in order to be the Savior of the world, Jesus was going to have to die—and she was going to have to watch. But she must have been thinking about this prophecy all the way home to Nazareth in Galilee.

What does it tell us about Jesus?

Now, I know these are supposed to be the joyful mysteries, but it's hard to think about the events surrounding the birth of Jesus without also remembering why he came to be one of us. He came to reconcile humanity to God, which requires something called *atonement*.

There are a lot of ways to think about atonement, but whenever we say that Jesus died for us, or that he died for our sins so that we could be saved, we're talking about the atonement. Maybe you've heard it like this: *he paid a debt he didn't owe because we owed a debt we couldn't pay*. Sin had separated humanity from God, and God wanted to get us back, because, after all, God loves us. But God is both merciful and just, and it would be against his nature for his mercy to diminish his justice, or for his justice to diminish his mercy. So, he came up with a solution to the problem of sin that expressed both his mercy and his justice. In his mercy, he extended his divinity into our world by sending the Son with his invitation of forgiveness. But justice required that humanity pay for the sins of humanity. And part of the reason Luke includes the account of Jesus' dedication in the Temple is to emphasize for us that he was willing to submit himself to the law. So the Son took on humanity to fulfill the law, and to take on the consequences of sin on our behalf. No mere human could absorb the consequences of sin for anyone else, because we all have sin of our own. Only a human who had no sin of his own could take that on. And so he became one of us in order to do what we could not do. *He paid a debt he didn't own because we owed a debt we couldn't pay.*

But as we've already seen, he could not be truly human without setting aside his omnipresence (to be contained by time and space) and his omnipotence (to accept the weakness of humanity). Here we see that Christ also could not be truly human without setting aside his omniscience, that attribute of the divine that is all-knowing. The paradox of the humble God is that the omniscient One was willing to submit to the law, defer to teachers, and even learn things.

I know it seems strange to think that Jesus, who is God as much as the Father and the Holy Spirit are God, had to learn things. But that's what Luke tells us. "The child grew and became strong, [becoming] filled with wisdom; and the favor of God was upon him" (Lk 2:40). Of course, in his divine nature, he never ceased to be omniscient, but in his humanity, he was "emptied" (Phil 2:6–7), that is, self-limited, so that he could experience real humanity. Although to be fair, as we'll see in the last of the joyful mysteries, he was ahead of the curve. He was filled with the Holy Spirit his whole life, so that he was able to learn quickly, and between the Holy Spirit and the teaching of his parents, he was able to figure out who he was. I do not believe that the newborn Jesus was conscious of the fullness of his mission while swaddled in the manger, though some theologians are reluctant to say that he had to grow in the consciousness of his divinity. In any case, Luke tells us that he grew in wisdom, until the day came when he was ready to call his disciples and begin his ministry. But even then, there were things he didn't know, because he voluntarily veiled his omniscience to live as a human. Speaking about the end of the age (and his Second Coming), Jesus admitted he did not know when that would be. He said, "But of that day and hour no one knows, neither the angels of heaven, nor the Son, but the Father alone" (Mt 24:36; Mk 13:32). The Father knows, but the Son doesn't. But just to be clear, his divine nature is not diminished by the Incarnation, so another way to say that would be that his divine nature knows, but his human nature doesn't. This is how most of the Church Fathers explained it. The point is the same. The divine Son of God was willing to live with the limitations of humanity.

Interestingly, in the early Church it wasn't the idea that Jesus learned things that got some people upset. It was the idea that he started out small, as a baby, and grew into an adult. How can a divine person grow, they asked? Some said that because he was born and grew up, that meant he could not be divine. These were the adoptionists, who denied Jesus' divinity and said that he was only the son of God in a purely human sense. Others said that because he was divine, he could not have ever been a baby. And *those* people wanted to chop off the beginning of Luke's gospel, and just start with Jesus' Baptism. These people belonged to one of several groups on the fringes of the Church, and we usually refer to them as gnostics (the "g" is silent). They went to the other extreme from the adoptionists and denied Jesus' real humanity. But you already know how the Church Fathers answered these heresies. They affirmed *both* of Jesus' two natures: his divinity and humanity. Although a divine human is another paradox, the Church Fathers knew that Christ's divinity does not rule out real humanity, and his humanity does not rule out true and full divinity.

Jesus is the divine Son of God. He didn't *need* to be dedicated in the Temple. It was not done for his sake, or even for Joseph and Mary. It was done to make a statement. He had become one of us, and he was beginning his life under the same constraints that we live with. He was going to experience what it meant to be limited, vulnerable, and sometimes even unsure (as we will see when we get to the Agony in the Garden). He was presented in the Temple to show that he was living under the law, like all of God's people. And when Simeon saw him, he said, "my eyes have seen your [God's] salvation." He saw the child Jesus and called him God's salvation. And the name Jesus (Joshua in Hebrew) means "God saves." In Jesus, salvation had come to God's people.

We see in the coming of Jesus a very clear message that he comes for all people. He came for Jews (Simeon and Anna) and Gentiles (magi); he came for rich (magi) and poor (shepherds), and he came for male (Joseph and Simeon) and female (Elizabeth and Anna). The Feast of the Presentation of the Lord, also called Candlemas, is celebrated forty days after the Nativity, on February 2. It is also now celebrated as the Feast of the Purification of Mary, though some of the early Church Fathers connected Mary's purification with the annunciation, or with her Immaculate Conception. They reasoned that she did not really need to be purified from the birth of Jesus in the way that Jewish tradition required a woman's purification. Incidentally, before there were ever any weather-predicting groundhogs, the tradition was that a sunny day (with the sun casting shadows) on February 2 meant a longer winter. A cloudy day on February 2 meant an early spring.

What aspects of this mystery should we imitate?

Sometimes we do things not because we need to but because others need us to. Jesus submitted to the law because there were reasons why it would be good for us. When God calls us to do something that's good for others, we must do it as a labor of love, rather than ask, "Why should I?" If the divine Word of God could accept humility to serve humanity, we can be ready to humble ourselves to serve others, too.

MEDITATION

Jesus is the humble God, the divine human, the all-powerful but self-limiting Savior.

5.

THE FINDING OF JESUS IN THE TEMPLE

The Paradox of Tough Love

What is the Finding of Jesus in the Temple?

Read Luke 2:41–52.

Luke tells us that Jesus was about twelve years old, so the year would have been about AD 7. Every year at the time of Passover, Joseph and Mary would make the journey from Nazareth in Galilee to Jerusalem for the festival. But this particular year something happened that would unnerve any parent. Jesus went missing.

Now you might wonder how a caravan could leave Jerusalem and travel for a whole day without parents noticing that their twelve-year-old son was not with them. But you have to remember that this was the caravan of an extended family, with a lot of people. It was one caravan among many, so it was probably like being in the middle of a large parade. All those cousins called the "brothers and sisters of the Lord" were probably with them, and they all had their own parents and extended families in the mix. No doubt all the parents of this extended family were used to co-parenting one another's kids. When you consider that they came from a relatively small town, you can imagine that it was quite common for parents not to see their twelve-year-old son all day but assume that he was safe among his many uncles, aunts, cousins, and trusted neighbors. It was probably only at the first nightfall on the road that Joseph and Mary started asking the others, "Have you seen Jesus?" Only then would the panic have set in, as one relative after another replied, "We haven't seen him all day."

So Mary and Joseph had to turn around and make a day's walk back to Jerusalem. Then it took them another full day to find Jesus. If we assume that the "three days" includes the first day on the road and the second day going back, then there were two nights when Jesus was not with his parents. Those must have been two very sleepless nights for Joseph and Mary.

Eventually, they found him, still in the Temple, impressing the Pharisees. We have no idea where he slept for those two nights, but at some point over those few days the conversation must have gone from Jesus asking questions to the Pharisees asking *him* questions, perhaps grilling him with harder and harder questions as he fired back answers full of surprising wisdom. This event foreshadows the conflict Jesus would later have with the Pharisees. And Luke tells us that he astounded them.

But when Joseph and Mary found him, they reprimanded him. "Why have you done this to us?" They had been worried sick. Now you might think that Mary's faith in God, and her knowledge of Jesus' identity, would have mitigated some of the normal fear. But when he replied that they should have known he would be in his Father's house, Luke tells us that they didn't know what he meant. In any case, he obediently left the Temple and went home with them.

This is the only story of Jesus we get between his infancy and his adulthood. There are several legendary (or *apocryphal*) accounts that include more stories of his childhood, but they are not historical. All we really know is what Luke tells us, that this story of Jesus at age twelve is part of his increasing wisdom, and presumably his increasing awareness of his own identity and mission. In fact, it's not a coincidence that the age of twelve is historically considered the age of accountability for young men, the age at which they are considered responsible for their own actions. In a religious context, twelve is the age at which young men are expected to claim the traditional faith as their own. Biologically, this is the age that the brain develops to the point where it can handle logic and abstract reasoning. So a person at this age is just beginning to understand things like symbolism, metaphors, and, well . . . theology. Later this would become the (approximate) age of the Bar Mitzvah.

Where was Mary?

Once again we find Mary in the dusty and chaotic streets of Jerusalem, as well as in the crowded Temple. The three days Jesus was separated from his parents also foreshadow his death, and that he rose on the third day. Mary, who lost Jesus in the city and found him in the Temple, would also lose him at the Cross and find him resurrected. The child who asked, "Why were you looking for me?" would be the crucified One about whom the angel would say, "Why do you seek the living one among the dead? He is not here, but he has been raised" (Lk 24:5–6).

Mary and Joseph must have panicked and been frustrated while looking for him. Any parent can relate to what it would feel like to lose track of a child for that much time, even if he's considered an adult. If you have known the anxieties of parenting, you may take comfort in knowing that Mary did too. And if you've known those struggles and frustrations, you may also relate to the extreme joy and relief felt by Mary and Joseph when their child was found and was safe. And yet, there are many parents who know the frustration without ever knowing the release of tension. They know the sorrow without ever knowing the relief. Some even have to bury their children. Mary knew this sorrow, too. She was willing to travel this road, even the road to the Cross, and to lose her Son, so that our sons and daughters could be saved for eternal life, even those who are lost to us in this life.

What does it tell us about Jesus?

The first thing we have to say is that nobody sinned here. Jesus lagging behind was not a sin. He did not disrespect his parents or act in a disobedient way. He simply got caught up in the conversation and didn't even realize they had left (remember that in his human life, there *were* some things he didn't know). But neither did Joseph and Mary sin by reprimanding the young Messiah. Their correction is an act of love, just as the discipline of any parent should be an act of love. We are told in scripture that even God disciplines those whom he loves. This is a mystery, and we tend not to assume that God punishes people in this life under the new covenant. Yet it is God's prerogative to show his omnibenevolent (always good) love in ways that might seem like *tough love* to us. So the mystery of finding Jesus in the Temple is the paradox of tough love. Sometimes parental love is tough love, and even when the child is innocent, sometimes tough love is necessary to protect the child from danger.

I once wrote and directed a Christmas musical for youth. But instead of starting with the Star of Bethlehem or the annunciation, the first scene was Joseph and Mary finding Jesus in the Temple at age twelve. The first spoken line was Joseph's: "You're in big trouble, young man!" But then Mary calms him, and as Joseph goes off to prepare for the journey home, the young Jesus asks his Mother, "Why am I so different from all the other kids?" The story of Christmas is a flashback as Mary explains to her Son his unique birth.

As I have often imagined it, there must have been a point at which Mary told Jesus about the circumstances surrounding his birth. She must have told him the stories of the annunciation by the archangel Gabriel, the Visitation to Elizabeth, his birth in Bethlehem, and his presentation in the Temple, perhaps even the surprising prophecies from Anna and Simeon. And as Jesus "grew in wisdom," he must have had a growing awareness of his unique relationship with God, his mission, and even his divinity. And this event—the discussion with the Pharisees in the Temple—must have been a significant step in that development. By the time he was ready to call his disciples, he knew exactly who he was and what he had come to do.

If you think about it this way, when Jesus says, "Did you not know that I must be in my Father's house?" he was starting a journey that would end with him coming full circle, back to the Temple, when he would throw out the money changers and say, "My house shall be a house of prayer, but you are making it a den of thieves" (Mt 21:12–13, Mk 11:15–17, Lk 19:45–46). Notice that for Jesus the Temple has gone from being "my Father's house" to being "my house." (In John 2:14–16, he does call it "my Father's house," but in John's gospel he is cleansing the Temple at the *beginning* of his ministry, not at the end, on his way to the Cross.)

Love is not always easy, or convenient. Sometimes it's downright painful. The paradox of God's omnibenevolent tough love is a model for love in the real world of our everyday life. Even Jesus had to walk the line between obedience and authority. Out of love he obeyed his parents. Out of love he criticized the Pharisees and others all throughout his ministry. Out of love he submitted himself to the law. Out of love he reinterpreted the law. And out of love he accepted the humiliating death of crucifixion. Every one of his actions echo his words, "Did you not know that I must be in my Father's house?" It's as if he was saying, "Did you not know that I must be doing my Father's work?" In fact, in John's gospel, he goes so far as to say, "The Father and I are one" (Jn 10:30).

This doesn't mean that the Father and the Son are one *and the same*. The Father is not the Son, and the Son is not simply the incarnation of the Father. Theologically, we can say that it means the Father and the Son share the same divine nature (also with the Holy Spirit). But it also means that the Son comes with the Father's authority, and with the Father's agenda, that the Father and Son always work together, and are always doing the same thing.

This doctrine is called *inseparable operation*. It means that all three persons of the Trinity are involved in all divine activity. There is no time when the Father, Son, and Spirit are off doing different things. And we cannot make distinctions between the persons of the Trinity based on function or activity, as if to say, for example, that the Father is the Creator, the Son is the Redeemer, and the Spirit is the Sanctifier. This is actually a heresy (called modalism), because the truth is that all three persons of the Trinity are Creator, all three persons are Redeemer, and all three are Sanctifier. One divinity means one power and one activity. All divine activity is done by the singular will and power of all three divine persons, and is motivated by love, because as John tells us, "God is love" (1 Jn 4:8). And God is always good. But love is sometimes tough love.

What aspects of this mystery should we imitate?

Tough love means doing the right thing for those we love, even when it's not easy, or not what they want from us. Tough love is love that is not watered down or manipulated. Tough love is a balancing act: respecting and serving our parents and other elders while maintaining healthy boundaries and identity; and giving our children all the advantages and blessings we can while still training them, disciplining them, and refusing to spoil them.

So Mary finds herself once again in the Temple with Jesus. Now he's almost a teenager, but we can imagine that the scare she got from losing him for three days, and the relief she felt from finding him, might have made her think back to his first trip to the Temple, when he was presented and dedicated as an infant. Mary and Joseph brought Jesus to worship, and made a tradition of it. It was part of their lifestyle. And so it should be for us, as we make worship a part of our life's rhythm and teach our children to do the same (Heb 10:25). Loving parents still find Jesus in the temple, but now in the tabernacle, and in the monstrance, and on the altar table. We, too, must find Jesus in the temple, by coming to receive his Body and Blood in the Holy Eucharist.

MEDITATION

God's love can be tough love, training us to be more holy. In the end, however, it is always merciful love.

PART 2

The Luminous Mysteries (Thursdays)

A Mystery in History: Praying the Rosary as a Form of Protest

Jesus refused to be a political Messiah, but that doesn't mean that he takes no interest in the injustice of empires. On several occasions, people praying the Rosary have brought freedom to nations, including Brazil and the Philippines. Historically, revolution is always bloody, and it is often anti-Christian. But praying the Rosary has proven to be a bloodless revolution for peace and justice throughout history.

When the leaders of Brazil were trying to convert the government there to communism (in the 1960s) and effectively to sell their people into Soviet slavery, the president publicly ridiculed the Catholic faith. In response, the clergy called for the people to pray the Rosary, and they did. Tens of thousands of people (mostly women) would gather and pray the Rosary aloud to disrupt communist rallies and propaganda. The movement soon grew to the hundreds of thousands. The government threatened military action, but no one was ever hurt, and eventually those trying to force communism on Brazil fled the country.

In the Philippines, in the 1980s, the president and first lady were accumulating riches and luxuries while their people were starving. When a candidate tried to run against the president, he was assassinated. When his widow ran against the president, the election was rigged, and the incumbent president showed his true colors as a dictator by taking over the military and the media. At this point the clergy called for a peaceful protest that included praying the Rosary (fueled by a Rosary crusade led by Fr. Patrick Peyton that drew millions of people), as well as holding prayer vigils and marches. The people responded faithfully, and within a week the soldiers laid down their arms and joined the protesters. The dictator was forced to flee the country, and the Philippines became a democracy.

6.

THE BAPTISM OF JESUS
The Paradox of an Unnecessary Necessity

What is the Baptism of Jesus?

Read John 1:19–34 (parallels in Matthew 3:11–17, Mark 1:7–11, and Luke 3:15–22).

We tend to think of our Baptism as having "washed away" our sins. And that's true: Baptism cleanses us of original sin, and all personal sin up until the time of the Baptism. But what Baptism takes away is only half the picture; Baptism also gives us something. It gives us grace, which is God's love, forgiveness, presence, and power that help us to live the life to which baptized Christians are called. But then why did Jesus have to be baptized? He had no sins to wash away, and he needed no grace because he is a Source of grace.

The truth is Jesus *didn't need* to be baptized. What Baptism does for us, in terms of taking away sin and giving us grace, is not what Baptism did for him. His Baptism was not like ours. Jesus' Baptism was the Baptism of John, which was a Baptism of cleansing based on repentance. But wait a minute. He didn't need to repent either. John himself recognized this, and said, *I should be baptized by you; what are you doing coming to me for Baptism?* So, what's going on here?

Well, it turns out that Jesus' Baptism did not take anything away from him or give him anything that he did not already have.

But his Baptism did do something for him, and it certainly did something for us.

So then, what did Jesus' Baptism do for him? Although he did not need to receive grace, we might think of Jesus' Baptism as his "ordination" for his public ministry. I am not saying that he first received the Holy Spirit at his Baptism. Even though the Holy Spirit anointed him at his Baptism, he was always the Anointed One (the Christ), and he always had the Holy Spirit. But we might say that at the moment of his Baptism, he was being commissioned by the Father, and anointed by the Holy Spirit, to begin his ministry. This set him on the path that would lead him to the Cross on our behalf.

What did Jesus' Baptism do for us? By submitting to Baptism, Jesus instituted the Christian Sacrament of Baptism. There were Jewish washings, and prophetic cleansings (such as John's), but there wasn't really anything like Christian Baptism before Jesus stepped into the water. In fact, by stepping into the water, and going down into it and under it, Jesus consecrated water as a sacramental element. So, just as Jesus instituted the Sacrament of the Eucharist at the Last Supper, he also instituted Christian Baptism by submitting to John's Baptism. And it is through our Baptism (and Confirmation) that Jesus offers us the indwelling of the Holy Spirit. John the Baptizer said that he himself only baptized with water, but Jesus' Baptism would be one in which he would baptize with the Holy Spirit.

It is important to note that our Baptism does not "baptize us into the Catholic Church" specifically. All Christian Baptisms, as long as they are done with water, in the name of the Father, Son, and Holy Spirit (Mt 28:19), baptize a person into the universal Church, the whole Body of Christ. Baptism is (and should be) the one thing that still unites all Christians, and in fact we say in our Creed that we believe in *one* Baptism, not many. Unfortunately, there are some Christian groups that exacerbate division by declaring infant Baptism invalid and/or by rebaptizing those who were previously (validly) baptized, but the ideal is that we are all baptized into the one universal Church.

Where was Mary?

When Jesus began his ministry, Mary must have been both extremely proud of her Son and afraid of what was to come—maybe like a mother who sends her son off to war or to the mission field. In fact, some early missionaries packed their belongings in their coffins, because they knew they were never coming back. Mary must have dreaded the day when Jesus would leave her house, leave his workshop, and set out to accomplish the mission of salvation.

The gospels don't actually mention Mary at this point in the story, but it seems reasonable that she might have been there with him on the day he was baptized. If she was, she might have heard the voice of God the Father—Jesus' "real" Father—saying that he was proud of Jesus. (Mark and Luke tell us that Jesus heard "*You* are my beloved Son . . . ," but Matthew tells us that the others who were there heard "*This* is my beloved Son . . .") Mary must have felt great joy, knowing that she had fulfilled her vocation of raising and teaching the Son of God. But she also must have remembered the prophecy of Simeon, and realized that on that very day Jesus was embarking on a mission that would lead him to the Cross and would be like a sword in her heart.

What does it tell us about Jesus?

Like Jesus' dedication when he was presented in the Temple, he didn't need or require Baptism. He did it to make a point: to show his relationship to the Father, that he is the Father's Son, and that his ministry and his Passion were all part of a mission on behalf of the Father. But he also submitted to Baptism in order to start something new. Before he performed his first miracle in Cana, before he gathered his disciples, before he healed anyone or taught anything, and even before his temptation in the desert, Jesus identified himself with a movement of people who were consecrating themselves to God. By doing that, he started the next phase of that movement: its fulfillment, really. And he instituted the sacrament by which all of his followers would be initiated into that movement, the movement that would be called his Church.

Jesus, however, was no ordinary leader, and certainly not a politician. Who was he? John the Baptizer tells us that he existed before him; the guy who was born six months after him existed before him! How is that possible? It is because, as John the apostle tells us at the beginning of his gospel, Jesus is the Incarnation—the embodiment—of the divine nature of God, who is eternal. So in the person of Jesus, God, who created time and space, has entered into time and space. The Creator entered creation. Not in a way that confuses the Creator with creation, or blurs the line between Creator and creation. Rather, the God who cannot be limited (except voluntarily) has taken on the limitations of humanity in order to become one of us, so that he could reconcile humanity to God.

The Baptizer announced that Jesus is "the Lamb of God who takes away the sin of the world." The people who heard him say that would probably have taken it as a strange combination of Passover (the Lamb, whose blood averts God's judgment) and the Day of Atonement (with the scapegoat, who takes away the sins of the people). This means that John the Baptizer was prophetically announcing that Jesus would take the sins of the world on himself (cf. Isaiah, chapter 53) so that those who identified with him could be forgiven. He would be a sacrifice and his blood would lead to the salvation of all those who put their trust in him. And those who put their trust in him would identify with him and with his Church, by being baptized.

The paradox of the Baptism of the Lord is the "unnecessary necessity." Jesus did not need the water. The water needed him. He is the Creator of the water who went down into the water. He came down into creation to see it from within, from the perspective of creatures like us, and to accept the limitations of our human condition, so that he could raise us up.

What aspects of this mystery should we imitate?

It's interesting that Matthew and Luke both tell us that the Baptizer said that Jesus would baptize with the Holy Spirit, *and fire.* What does it mean to baptize with fire?

The Holy Spirit is God, but he is that person of the Trinity who we believe indwells us. St. Paul said that our bodies are temples of the Holy Spirit (1 Cor 6:19). Baptism with the Holy Spirit is the gift of the Holy Spirit, which is the gift of God's presence within us. And that presence comes with fire.

Now, fire is a metaphor. Sometimes in the Bible it refers to destruction, but in this case it refers to purification. The Old Testament uses the image of the fire of the crucible (the refiner's fire that purifies precious metals) as a metaphor for purification. See for example, Psalm 12:7, 66:10; Zechariah 13:8–9; and Malachi 3:2–4. In the New Testament, St. Peter would write, "For a little while you have had to suffer various trials, so that the genuineness of your faith—being more precious than gold that, though perishable, is tested by fire—may be found to result in praise and glory and honor when Jesus Christ is revealed" (1 Pt 1: 6–7, NRSV).

Of course, we should be baptized, and we should baptize our children, initiating them into the family of God in the Church, and giving them the gift of God's grace and the presence of the Holy

Spirit. But Baptism is not the end of something; it's the beginning. Jesus said that the branches that didn't bear fruit would be cut off, and that even those branches that do bear fruit would be pruned (Jn 15:2). This pruning is the same thing as the refining fire of the Holy Spirit. The very presence of the Holy Spirit in our lives purifies and "declutters" us to make us more efficient at living the gospel. So we cannot afford to rest on our Baptism as though that's all we need. We imitate this mystery by counting our Baptism as our own commissioning for the mission God has for us in this life, living the life of a baptized Christian, growing in faith, and submitting to the pruning away of whatever we have in our lives that prevents us from bearing fruit.

MEDITATION

Jesus' Baptism was not necessary for him, but it was necessary for us. By stepping into the water, he sanctified it as a sacramental element and made it a vehicle for new life. And Jesus entering water, which is both a basic element of nature and a sacramental element of the Church, is a beautiful image of the Creator entering creation.

7.

THE WEDDING AT CANA

The Mundane Made Holy

What is the Wedding at Cana?

Read John 2:1–11.

The story of the Wedding at Cana is only in the Gospel of John, but John makes a point to tell us that Jesus turning the water into wine was the first of his "signs." He calls them signs (rather than simply saying "miracles") because each miraculous thing that Jesus did points beyond itself to a greater truth. Just as Jesus sanctified water by being baptized, here he sanctifies wine, which will become one of the elements of the Sacrament of the Eucharist. He also blesses the fellowship of a party and a family reunion by providing for the joy and conversation that wine is intended to enhance. Later in his ministry there would come a time when he would be asked to talk about the kingdom of heaven, and he would compare it to a wedding reception (Mt 22:1–14). And at the Last Supper, he would tell his disciples that he would not drink wine again until he shared it with them in the kingdom (Mt 26:29). Jesus knew how to have fun, and it seems he was promising us that heaven will be like a party, a family reunion!

At the wedding in Cana, Jesus also sanctified the Sacrament of Marriage, though matrimony would not become an official sacrament until later in the history of the Church. Even though he would not be married himself, Jesus validated marriage as a vocation, and blessed it. But just like water, wine was a very mundane thing back then. It was something people drank every day. In fact, at some times and in some places in the Roman Empire, wine could be cheaper than clean water. Weddings were not an everyday thing, but they were regular celebrations that punctuated the year of any community. They were a familiar part of life: something to look forward to and something that brought a family and a community together.

Jesus made it a part of his mission to bless the ordinary and make it holy. This is not to say that everything is holy, since holiness has to do with being set apart, or set aside, for God. What is holy is to be used to worship God, to bring the people into a closer relationship with God, and to remind us regularly of our relationship with God. Holy things are not to be taken for granted or disrespected. Not everything can be holy, for if everything it holy, then nothing is. But ordinary things *can* be holy, when they are part of the natural rhythms of life that God has given us, and when we recognize that in gratitude.

Jesus, in his ministry and in his parables, sanctified and held up the holiness of planting, and harvesting, and fishing, and childbirth, and weddings. He sanctified the mundane, not by proclaiming some vague notion that everything is holy, but by turning the routine of life in the first century into a holy rhythm of repentance and celebration, of mourning and dancing (see Psalm 30).

Where was Mary?

Mary was Jesus' "plus one." Or maybe it was the other way around. The bride and/or the groom were obviously known to Jesus' family, and the disciples were there, too. It was only a few days after Jesus had called his disciples, so this is truly one of the first things they did together, as a group: they all went to a wedding. Cana is less than two hours' walk from Nazareth.

You know the story: the hosts were running out of wine, and it seemed as though the party would end early. This would probably have been quite embarrassing to the family. Mary pointed out the wine shortage to Jesus, and he said to her, *What does that have to do with me?* This was not said in a disrespectful or dismissive way. I imagine that Jesus knew full well what he was about to do, and that he said this with a smirk, or a twinkle in his eye. And then he said, "My hour has not yet come."

Maybe it seems strange to us that Mary would be the one to say when it was time for Jesus to truly begin his ministry. But after all, he had already gathered his disciples, so in some sense he must have said to them, "It's time to begin." And in any case, why shouldn't it be Mary whose word sets things in motion? It was her word, her *fiat*, that set everything in motion at the annunciation. Well, Mary didn't give up, and you know how the story ends: Jesus performed his first miracle, revealing his glory. This solidified the disciples' faith in him, and they were off and running.

Although it appears that Jesus was a bit reluctant to intervene, he acted based on Mary's intercession. And so we see Mary as intercessor on behalf of her people. In fact, this story demonstrates Mary's role in the Church. The faithful who put their trust in Mary and in her Son whisper their petitions in her ear. She takes them to her Son. And to the Church, she points to Jesus and says, "Do whatever he tells you."

What does it tell us about Jesus?

The Christian faith has never been one that elevates the spiritual so much that it debases the physical. Although St. Paul and others caution us about the *desires* of the flesh, still the ultimate manifestation of our salvation will be the resurrection of our bodies, entering into the eternal kingdom of heaven. We were never meant to be spirits only. We were created to be embodied, and our redemption is redemption of both the body and the spirit. And so the Son of God became fully human, with all of its physicality (and the limitations that come with that) in order to redeem and glorify our full humanity. This tells us that God does not discount the physical; the things of the material world are part of God's good creation and are not meant to be treated as disposable. In fact, in the person of Jesus Christ, God was using the material things of the world to bring us back to him and teach us to love our neighbors. In the very Incarnation of Jesus, physical creation itself is sanctified, because the Word of God became physical. And just as his divinity sanctified his humanity, by extension he offers salvation and sanctification to all who share in his human nature.

On at least one occasion, Jesus even used mud and spit to heal a man's eyes (see John, chapter 9). Think about that, any time you are tempted to think of Jesus in terms that separate him from us. He could have healed the man with a word, or even a thought. He could have waved his hand over the man's eyes like a Jedi. But he didn't. He intentionally healed the man in a way that would remind everyone of how we were made (see Genesis 2:7): out of mud and water. But that's not to say we are worthless. By doing this, Jesus made the earth and the water of infinite value to that man who was given his sight. And he would do the same with wine at the wedding. And later with wine mixed with water, and bread at the institution of the Eucharist.

So we as Christians must not fall into the ancient mistake of the gnostics, who taught that the things of the material world are beneath us. We do not separate the material from the spiritual in that way. We are embodied spirits, not spirits trapped in shells that are to be discarded.

One other thought: It turns out that Jesus makes the best wine. I don't think we can dismiss this little detail of the story as though it's simply a cute punch line meant to make us smile at the divinity of Christ. It's more than that; it is another sign, or another aspect of the sign of the wedding at Cana. And it points to the fact that in Jesus, the best is saved for last. The last will be first, and the first will be last (see Matthew 19:30, 20:16; Mark 10:31; Luke 13:30). This means that those you think are closest to God and his kingdom might not be—and those you consider the farthest from God and from his kingdom might be closer that you think. So the people whom we may be tempted to shun because of their physical bodies or their material situations might be exactly the people who are even closer to God than we are.

Jesus began his ministry at a wedding. And he told a parable that described the kingdom of heaven as being like a wedding banquet, what the book of Revelation calls the Wedding of the Lamb. The gospels and the book of Revelation, the beginning and end of the Good News in the New Testament, are like the bookends of the work of Christ. His first miracle was at a wedding, and his last will be the resurrection that will bring us into the eternal wedding banquet in the kingdom.

What aspects of this mystery should we imitate?

Therefore, as Christians we are called to engage in the corporal works of mercy to love our neighbors by caring for the bodies, and the physical well-being, of our neighbors. At the wedding in Cana, Jesus sanctified the physical and affirmed the goodness of the mundane. To imitate this mystery is to make a point to attend to the rhythm of repentance and celebration in life, and to make room in our rhythm of life for the corporal works of mercy, such as feeding the hungry, offering hospitality to the homeless, caring for the sick and the dying, and giving comfort to the prisoner.

In the story, it took the cooperation of the wine stewards to actually make the wine. They had to get the water and fill the jars. And that's how God does things. God works very often through what we call *synergy*, that is, the cooperation of people who are willing to work along with God's grace, tapping into that grace as empowerment to do the will of God in the world.

MEDITATION

Jesus makes everyday things holy, and he gives us permission to sanctify the rhythm of our lives by punctuating our days, weeks, months, and years with cycles of repentance and celebration.

8.

THE PROCLAMATION OF THE KINGDOM

The Paradox of Now and Not Yet

What is the Proclamation of the Kingdom?

Since this mystery is not just one event in the life of Jesus, there are a lot of scripture passages one could read to meditate on it. Many of Jesus' parables begin with him saying, "The kingdom is like this . . ." For now let's focus on two of them: following on the mystery of the miracle at a wedding, read the parable of the wedding banquet, Matthew 22:1–14, and the parable of the ten bridesmaids, Matthew 25:1–13.

The kingdom of God (or kingdom of heaven in Matthew's gospel) is the core of Jesus' preaching. Everything he said and did revolved around, and pointed to, this reality. So what exactly is the kingdom? Those of us who grew up in a world colonized by Western Europe have this vague idea about kingdoms, along with kings, and queens, and knights. But for Jesus, the idea of "kingdom" is not one kingdom among many, but one overarching kingdom. So it would be fair to translate this concept as the Empire of God. And in fact, that's how Jesus' audience would have heard it, because they lived as colonized people under the Roman Empire. So on one level, the kingdom of God is the empire of God, as opposed to the empire of Rome. We can understand why some people might have expected Jesus to be a political Messiah, and revolutionary leader, but that was exactly what he refused to be, because as Jesus himself said, "My kingdom is not from this world" (Jn 18:36, NRSV).

And yet, the kingdom is not completely other-worldly. There is an aspect of the kingdom that is *in* this world, if not *of* this world. Jesus told the Pharisees "the kingdom of God is among you" (Lk 17:21). He may have been referring to himself, or to his mission, but either way, the point is that by coming into the world, he was bringing the kingdom of God with him.

As it turns out, there are two aspects to the kingdom, or empire, of God. It is here among us, but it is still yet to come. God's kingdom is in our hearts; it is in us, but someday we will be in it. Now, it is concealed, but the day will come when it will be revealed. And in many ways, this *revealing* or "revelation" of the kingdom is what the book of Revelation is all about.[1]

When Jesus came the first time, he brought with him the kingdom, but it remains concealed, like a seed under soil. When Jesus comes at the end of time, that is, when he returns at his "Second Coming," he will bring the kingdom of God in its fully revealed sense. So the kingdom is now, but it is also not yet. And we are called to live the values of the kingdom, even while we live in the world. Jesus' proclamation of the kingdom is his offer of forgiveness and reconciliation with God, and his call to repentance (conversion). Our response is to accept his invitation by living as citizens of the kingdom in the here and now when the kingdom is concealed, while we wait for the kingdom to be fully revealed.

Where was Mary?

It's probably safe to assume that Mary was with Jesus much of the time during his ministry. Mary is presented to us as one of a group of women who followed and supported Jesus (tradition makes her the leader of that group of women, which makes sense). So it's probably also safe to assume that Mary was aware of Jesus' miracles and heard most, if not all, of Jesus' preaching.

But I want to take that a step further and ask the question, Where did he get the ideas for his homilies? Of course, we assume that his divine unity with the Trinity and his unique relationship with the Father meant that he received his messages directly from the Father through the Spirit. After all, his parables make it clear that he is the Father's messenger, bringing the Father's message to humanity. And of course, we also assume that simply on a human level Jesus was extraordinarily smart, if only because he had no sin to get in the way of his intellect. On some occasions he affirms that he speaks on his own authority.

But having said all that, it is also true that he had to learn some things. His true humanity means that he had set aside certain qualities, such as omniscience, in the Incarnation. After all, you can't really experience the human condition if you're all-knowing (let alone omnipresent!). If this is hard for you to accept, remember that God cannot die, and yet the second person of the Trinity voluntarily took on a self-limitation so that he *could* die—for us. That self-limitation meant that in his humanity he didn't know everything. In fact, he admitted as much, when he said he did not know when his Second Coming would be (Mt 24:36; Mk 13:32). Remember that after the finding in the Temple incident, Luke tells that us he grew in wisdom (Lk 2:52).

So I would like to suggest that, in addition to his access to the Father and the Holy Spirit, and in addition to his own intellectual and prophetic powers, Jesus had teachers. And his first teacher was Mary. As I imagine it, there came a day when she had to sit him down and tell him about the circumstances surrounding his birth, as well as all she understood about how he fit into God's plan for the people of Israel. Mary had "kept all these things, reflecting on them in her heart" (Lk 2:19) so that she could pass them on to Jesus, and in that way, contribute to his own self-understanding, and to his understanding of his mission in the world.

What does it tell us about Jesus?

One point has to be clarified: The most important thing is not what Jesus said; it's who Jesus is. Jesus preached about a way that leads to salvation, but the point is that Jesus *is* the way. Jesus preached about truth, but he *is* truth incarnate, and the Source of all truth. Jesus preached about eternal life in God's kingdom, but he *is* the life, and he is the door into that kingdom (Jn 10:7). With his advent, now more than two thousand years ago, he inaugurated the kingdom of God, and brought it among us, and into us—yet it remains concealed. With his Second Coming, some day in the future, he will reveal the kingdom of God in such a way that all of creation will be renewed, so that "at the name of Jesus, every knee should bend . . . and every tongue confess that Jesus Christ is Lord, to the glory of God the Father" (Phil 2:10–11).

The parable of the wedding banquet is an allegory, in which the king represents God. The prince, of course, represents Jesus, and that makes him the groom. In the parable of the ten bridesmaids (Mt 25:1–13) too, the groom in the story represents Jesus, and the fact that the bridesmaids are waiting for the groom to return is analogous to the way that we are now in a time of waiting for Jesus to return. What's going on in the story is that the bride and groom are engaged, and the wedding will take place when the groom comes to town. They don't know when that will be, so they have to be ready.

So for us, it's as though Jesus' coming two thousand years ago was the "engagement." Jesus, the Groom, became engaged to his Church, and now we are in a time in between the engagement and the wedding. St. Paul picks up on this idea when he also makes the analogy of marriage as an image of the relationship between Christ and the Church (Eph 5:32). Jesus, Paul, and John in the book of Revelation all use this analogy of the union of Christ and his Church as a marriage, and of the kingdom of God as a wedding. The Church is the Bride of Christ. And we live in the time of faithful waiting, for when the Groom will return, and the kingdom will be fully revealed.

What aspects of this mystery should we imitate?

The point of the parable of the ten bridesmaids is to spend the engagement period in a state of readiness for the wedding: do not become complacent or lazy, but actively look for the return of the Groom. And so we live in this age as people who are attentive to the things that will endear our Groom to us when he returns. We live according to the values of the kingdom, as Jesus preached, even though we're not in the kingdom yet.

We may not be in the kingdom yet, but the kingdom is within us, and so there is an expectation that although we are *in* the world, we are not to be *of* the world (see John 17:14–18). How do we do that? By staying awake and keeping our lamps lit—in other words, living lives that don't ignore God but rather regularly show our gratitude to God in worship. That means keeping faithful to attend Mass, for after all, the word *Eucharist* means "thanksgiving," and we go to Mass to express our thanksgiving. I suppose that's just one reason we go to Mass, but if it were the only reason, it would be enough. By going to Mass we are not just *thinking* we are grateful and not just *saying* we are grateful but also *acting* grateful, and demonstrating our gratitude by the commitment of action.

MEDITATION

The core of Jesus' teaching is a reality that is both here now and not here yet. It is concealed in us, but someday it will be revealed and we will be in it. The kingdom is a seed planted in our hearts, a seed that we must plant in the world. But it will not be fully grown until Jesus returns.

9.

THE TRANSFIGURATION
The Paradox of Hidden Glory

What is the Transfiguration?

Read Luke 9:27–36 (parallels in Matthew 16:28–17:9, and Mark 9:1–10).

When "the Word became flesh," the divine Son of God came to live a human life, with all of its limitations. That means that he had to set aside certain aspects of divinity that would prevent him from being truly human, such as being all-powerful. Don't get me wrong, we are not saying that Jesus set aside his divinity. He remained fully divine throughout the whole of his life on earth (and there's no such thing as being "partially divine" anyway). And we are not even saying that he was without the divine attribute of omnipotence, because that's part of the very definition of divinity. But in order to be truly human, he "emptied himself" (Phil 2:7), which means that he voluntarily set aside his access to certain attributes of divinity in order to truly experience the frailty and vulnerability of the human condition.

All that is to say that in Jesus' life on earth, his glory (that is, the manifestation of his divinity) was concealed, much like the kingdom is concealed. It was present on earth by virtue of his coming, but it could only be seen with the eyes of faith. It was in the hearts of believers, but it was veiled from those who did not believe. And yet, for a brief moment, Jesus' glory was seen with the eyes of the flesh. His glory was revealed to Peter, James, and John, who witnessed this event we call the Transfiguration. And later, when John wrote his gospel, he followed the words "And the Word became flesh and made his dwelling among us" with "and we saw his glory, the glory as of the Father's only Son, full of grace and truth" (Jn 1:14).

Jesus had told his disciples that there were some among them who would "not taste death before they see the kingdom of God." Did that mean that Jesus was going to return for his Second Coming, unveiling the fully revealed kingdom within their lifetimes? Apparently not. In fact, Matthew, Mark, and Luke all tell us that within a week of Jesus saying this, three of the disciples did see— for a moment—the revealed glory of Jesus; they did get a glimpse into the heavenly realm. They saw the kingdom of God (or "the Son of Man coming in his kingdom," as Matthew has it) by a momentary unveiling of Jesus' glory. This is called the Transfiguration, because his appearance was changed. Transfiguration means a change in appearance, and Matthew and Mark actually say that he was "transfigured" using the Greek word *metamorphosis*. The appearance of his face changed (we don't really know how), and his clothes became dazzling white, which I take to mean that he became a *source* of light.

Where was Mary?

Mary was not there on the Mount of Transfiguration. But it's fair to say that Peter, James, and John learned something that day that Mary already knew. She had been privileged to "behold his glory" in her own special way when she was overshadowed by the Holy Spirit and became pregnant with the Son of God. She was among the first to see his face at his birth, and no one was in a better position than she was to appreciate how his appearance changed as he grew up and became a man. I venture to say that

Mary did not need to be present at the Transfiguration, because she already understood everything that it revealed. Think about the paradox of concealed glory. It was not hidden from Mary, but even the apostles found it difficult to see. How sad it is that the lack of faith makes it hard for so many people to see.

What does it tell us about Jesus?

When we think of the Transfiguration, we often imagine Jesus glowing. As I said above, the fact that he is described as having "dazzling white" clothes means that he became a *source* of light. This is significant. It's not simply that he was glowing, but that what was being revealed here was the fact that Jesus Christ, as the divine Son of God, is not a receiver but a Source. He did not *receive* creation as someone who comes into being (he is "begotten, not made"). Rather, he is the *agent* of creation, which means that it was through him that the Father created the universe ("all things were made through him"). He did not *receive* the gift of life; he is the *Source* of life. He does not *receive* light; he is the *Source* of light.

However, we should not imagine the Transfiguration as a vision of a disembodied Jesus. The gospels are not saying that he was without a body, or that he was transcending the body in some way. The gospels mention his clothes specifically to tell us that he was still embodied. Even later, when Jesus was raised from death, he would be embodied. The gospel writers all make it a point to be very clear about the fact that his was a bodily resurrection, not simply the appearance of a ghostly spirit. To some extent the Transfiguration gives us hints about Jesus' Resurrection, and by extension our own resurrection into the kingdom of heaven. Still, we must remember that even in his glory, Jesus' whole personhood includes his humanity. He became human to redeem and glorify human nature, not to show us how to shed our humanity.

Now what are we to make of the fact that Peter, James, and John saw Jesus talking with Moses and Elijah? Luke tells us that the three of them were talking about the fulfillment of Jesus' mission: the upcoming events of Jesus' Death, Resurrection, and Ascension. Some of the Church Fathers said that the appearance of Moses and Elijah are symbolic: Moses represents the law and Elijah represents the prophets, and so together they represent the Old Testament putting its stamp of approval on Jesus. Certainly it is true that Jesus fulfilled the Old Testament prophecies, but he also went beyond them, and redefined them. At the very least, this episode puts Jesus in the middle of the Old Testament patriarchs and New Testament apostles. His life is the turning point in the history of God's relationship with his people.

What aspects of this mystery should we imitate?

Peter, always the one to go out on a limb, spoke up. He said, "It is good for us to be here," and then volunteered to start building shelters for Jesus, Moses, and Elijah to stay in. His enthusiasm was misguided, though, because Moses and Elijah were not going to be sticking around. Mark and Luke want us to cut Peter some slack, and they tell us that he was so nervous he didn't know what he was saying. But I think what Peter was trying to do was make the experience last. He was having a "mountaintop" experience (in this case, literally), and he didn't want it to end. I think we can all relate to that, and yet we often don't make the time for those experiences.

To imitate this mystery, we must make a point to set aside time for getting away from the noise of everyday life, so that we can spend time with Jesus. We need to do this on an annual, monthly, weekly, and daily basis. Perhaps we might plan to participate in a parish retreat or other similar experience once a year. Maybe we could spend some time in Eucharistic Adoration once a month, or even once a week or more. We can at least try to make time for personal prayer and devotion once a day, or if we can't do it once a day, then perhaps once a week. We must set aside time to read scripture, pray—and of course pray the Rosary! Maybe you're already doing this. Wherever you are in the process of spiritual growth, ask yourself how you might step it up a bit, to create a daily, weekly, monthly, and yearly rhythm of life that is punctuated with opportunities to "behold his glory." And then do what the voice of the Father advises: "Listen to him!"

MEDITATION

Jesus reveals more of himself to us when we get away from the distractions of the world and find a quiet place to focus on him. His transfiguration is one time that he reveals his glory to us, foreshadowing the day when we will see him "face to face," and know him as well as he knows us (1 Cor 13:12).

10.

THE INSTITUTION OF THE EUCHARIST

The Paradox of Seeing the Invisible

What is the Institution of the Eucharist?

Read Matthew 26:26–28 (parallels in Mark 14:22–24 and Luke 22:15–20). Also read Luke 24:30–35 and 1 Corinthians 11:23–26.

At the Last Supper, Jesus created the Church. He did this by gathering his followers around a table and initiating the Sacrament of the Eucharist. And before there was anything like a church *building*, before the Church was an institution with religious orders and Catholic Charities, the Church was the faithful at the table. Jesus promised that whenever we gather in his name, he is with us (see Matthew 18:20). That promise is kept and fulfilled whenever we gather and "do this in remembrance of" him.

St. Paul would make it clear that this is no mere memorial, though, since disrespecting the Eucharist can actually drive you further from God, rather than bring you closer (see 1 Corinthians 11:27–33). From the very beginning of eucharistic theology—that is, from the first Church Fathers who explained the meaning of the sacrament down to the present day—the teaching of the Church is that what we receive is no longer bread and wine. Through the consecration, they have become the Body and Blood of Jesus—not in a merely symbolic or metaphorical way but really and truly the

Body and Blood of Christ. The same Body of Christ that was born in Bethlehem, that sojourned in Egypt, that grew up in Nazareth, that died and rose in Jerusalem—that same Body of Christ is made truly present on every altar at every Mass.

But in order to receive the real Body and Blood of Jesus in the Eucharist, we have to be willing to see them with the eyes of faith. For the senses of our bodies, the elements retain the aspects of bread and wine. They look like bread and wine, they taste like bread and wine, they feel like bread and wine, they smell like bread and wine, and if you could hear the breaking and pouring, they would even sound like bread and wine. But after the words of consecration, that is, after the presider quotes the words of Jesus over them, "this is my body" and "this is my blood," they are no longer bread and wine in their essence. Their essence (the theological term is *substance*) has become the substance of the Body and Blood of Christ. The Body and Blood of Christ, while truly present, are invisible, so they can only be perceived by faith. It is this that really matters because it is this that is of benefit to us.

Where was Mary?

Da Vinci's portrait notwithstanding, it's highly unlikely that everyone at the Last Supper was seated on only one side of the table. It's also highly unlikely that the twelve disciples were the only ones there with Jesus that night. It is probable that the group of women who followed and supported Jesus were also there, if only to serve at the meal. In any case, Mary was likely there. She was probably there to hear Jesus say that one of the disciples would betray him, and to hear all the disciples say, "Surely, not I, Lord?" She was probably aware of what was going on when Judas got up and left. She knew that whatever was going to happen was going to be a like a sword piercing her heart, and she was likely there to hear Jesus say, "I tell you, from now on I shall not drink this fruit of the vine until the day when I drink it with you new in the kingdom of my Father" (Mt 26:29).

And so Mary was there for that first Eucharist; she heard her Son proclaim the beginning of a new covenant with God. This was the new covenant that was promised by the prophet Jeremiah, when he said,

> The days are surely coming, says the LORD, when I will make a new covenant with the house of Israel and the house of Judah. It will not be like the covenant I made with their ancestors when I took them by the hand to bring them out of the land of Egypt—a covenant that they broke, though I was their husband, says the LORD. But this is the covenant that I will make with the house of Israel after those days, says the LORD: I will put my law within them, and I will write it on their hearts; and I will be their God, and they shall be my people. (Jer 31:31–33, NRSV)

We have already seen how Mary is the Ark of the New Covenant. Just as the Ark of the Old Covenant was the vessel that held the words of God on the stone tablets of Moses, Mary's womb was the vessel that held the Word of God and brought him into the world in his incarnation. The body of Jesus that was formed in the womb of Mary is the same Body and Blood of Christ that is made present on the altar of the Eucharist, the one we receive at every Mass.

What does it tell us about Jesus?

We cannot understand the true significance of the Eucharist without looking at what Jesus said about it, which is recorded in the sixth chapter of John's gospel. There we read what Jesus was teaching in the synagogue at Capernaum. He was addressing a Jewish audience that included some people who were disciples of his, and some who were not. He told them that he is the bread of life, and his Eucharist is bread from heaven. When they questioned him, he said,

> Unless you eat the flesh of the Son of Man and drink his blood, you do not have life within you. Whoever eats my flesh and drinks my blood has eternal life, and I will raise him up on the last day. For my flesh is true food and my blood is true drink. Whoever eats my flesh and drinks my blood remains in me, and I in him. Just as the living Father sent me, and I have life because of the Father, so also the one who feeds on me will have life because of me. This is the bread that came down from heaven. Unlike your ancestors who ate and still died, whoever eats this bread will live forever. (Jn 6:53–58)

When he said, "my flesh is *true* food, and my blood is *true* drink," he was saying that this is not a metaphor; he was not simply using bread and wine as a symbol. He meant that his followers were going to literally eat his body and drink his blood. And we can see that they understood him correctly, because many people took the opportunity to give up on him. Even some who were following him as disciples left him after he said these things (Jn 6:66). It seems that this was the moment that Judas decided to betray him (v. 71). Apparently, this teaching of Jesus was what made Judas give up all hope of him being a revolutionary. Even Judas now realized that was not the kind of messiah Jesus was going to be. He was not going to raise an army and drive out the Romans. He was not going to change the world. He was going to change hearts from the inside, and prepare them for the kingdom: the kingdom that is *not* of this world.

What was bad news for Judas is good news for us, because if Jesus had been just another revolutionary, he might have driven out the Romans; he might have become an earthly King of the Jews. But empires come and go, and if Jesus had created an earthly empire, it would mean nothing to us now except that it would be a different chapter in the history books. But the good news is that the kingdom Jesus established transcends history, and the Eucharist he instituted transcends time. So when we receive the Eucharist, we are not just participating in something that is here today and gone tomorrow. We are participating in something eternal. We are communing at the table of the Church with all those who have gone before us, and all those who will come after us. We share the same Eucharist with Mary and the disciples who were in the Upper Room; we share it with the saints of the Church and with our beloved ancestors. And in it, we are all promised a share in the heavenly banquet, when we will drink of the cup with Jesus himself in his Father's kingdom.

What aspects of this mystery should we imitate?

Luke tells us about two disciples who met the risen Jesus on the road to Emmaus. We're not exactly sure where Emmaus was, but Luke tells us it was about seven miles (or about seven and a half miles, according to the Greek) from Jerusalem. This means that Jesus had two or three hours' walking time to talk with these disciples, and all the while they did not recognize him. But when they got to Emmaus, they invited Jesus to stay with them for a meal, and at that meal, he broke the bread. In the breaking of the bread, they recognized him for who he really was. And so it is: Jesus is made known to us in the breaking of the bread. We recognize him in the Eucharist, not simply as a symbol, but in his powerful presence.

Recent polls tell us that many Catholics no longer believe in the real presence of Jesus Christ in the Eucharist. To imitate this mystery is not only to attend Mass and receive the Eucharist but also to do as the disciples of Emmaus. Luke tells us, "That same hour they got up and returned to Jerusalem," and told the others about their experience in the presence of the risen Christ and how they recognized him in the breaking of the bread. We, too, should "get up" from the table and tell others about our experience. We should never let our fellow Catholics be unsure about the real presence, and the grace that comes to us from receiving his Body and Blood.

MEDITATION

We recognize Jesus in the breaking of the bread. But his Body and Blood can only be seen with the eyes of faith.

PART 3

The Sorrowful Mysteries (Tuesdays and Fridays)

A Mystery in History: The Hiroshima Survivors

In August of 1945, the United States ended the war with Japan by dropping the world's first atomic bombs on the cities of Hiroshima and Nagasaki. In Hiroshima alone, more than 100,000 people were killed in an instant, and as many as 100,000 more died soon after from the effects of radiation. But at least four men (some accounts say eight), who were within a mile of ground zero, survived. To this day, no one can explain why, except to say that it was a miracle.

Eight Jesuit priests were living in a house in Hiroshima, where they prayed the Rosary every day. And for the rest of their lives (which they lived without any negative effects of the blast or the radiation) they were convinced that their commitment to Our Lady, and to praying her Rosary, is the reason they survived. Photographs of Hiroshima after the bombing show the city leveled, with the exception of the house where the Jesuits prayed the Rosary and the nearby church. Those buildings remained partially intact, and again, no one can give any scientific explanation why (though some say that the house had been reinforced against earthquakes).

No one can say for sure why some people are spared in a moment of great loss of life. But we do believe that the intercession of Mary and the saints can protect those who are devoted to Mary and her Son. Survivors who prayed the Rosary give credit to Mary's intercession, even though they could not have seen tragedy coming, and could not have known what to pray for.

11.

THE AGONY IN THE GARDEN
The Paradox of Two Wills in One Person

What is the Agony in the Garden?

Read Matthew 26:36–56 (parallels in Mark 14:32–50 and Luke 22:40–53) and John 12:27–36, 18:1–14.

After Jesus' Last Supper with his disciples, in which he instituted the Sacrament of the Eucharist, he went outside to a garden on the Mount of Olives, a garden called Gethsemane. Luke and John tell us that this was a habit of his, going out to the garden after dinner to pray. In fact, that's how Judas knew where to find him. Matthew and Mark both tell us that Jesus ended the Last Supper by singing a hymn, and after the hymn, he led the disciples out to the garden to pray.

The agony refers to Jesus' prayer in the garden, but you can think of it as encompassing the whole experience in Gethsemane, including his arrest. Apparently, Jesus' human nature was tempted, and he prayed for a way to finish his ministry without the Cross. He prayed that the Father might find another way to save humanity, maybe thinking of the way God had provided a substitute for Isaac, so that he did not have to be sacrificed. But no, Jesus knew that *he* was the substitute. He was the lamb who was to be sacrificed for our forgiveness, and our salvation. He struggled, but he did not sin. It's not a sin to be weak; that is a natural part of the human condition, and Jesus was (and still is) fully human.

This is one of those places in the gospels where the authors make it a point to give us details that remind us of Jesus' humanity, because it is in his humanity that he is one of us, that he is in solidarity with us. Here we see that he prayed so hard that he was sweating, and the sweat turned to blood. We know that Jesus felt pain and anguish, and that he cried. Here in the garden, anticipating his arrest, humiliation, torture, and slow execution, he must have experienced the culmination of his human emotions. And to add insult to the agony, his closest three disciples had fallen asleep.

Jesus' agony was not really over his impending death, though. He was going to give his life voluntarily; no one could take it from him against his will because of his divinity. And he was resolved to fulfill his mission, so it's not as though he was considering backing out. In fact, when Satan tried to tempt him to take the shortcut, he didn't take the bait, and when Peter suggested that he shouldn't have to die, he called Peter Satan! No, Jesus' agony was mostly (I think) sorrow over the sin of the world and over the fate of humanity if he didn't follow through. He didn't sweat, bleed, and cry for himself; it was all for us. In the end, though, Jesus finished his prayer by affirming his commitment to do the Father's will, even if his human will hoped, for a moment, that there could be another way.

In the gospels, when Jesus prays to the Father "not my will, but yours be done" (see Luke 22:42), the text uses the same word, *fiat* in Latin, that was used when Mary said her "yes" to God. So Jesus' "yes" parallels Mary's "yes." And just as Mary's "yes" reversed Eve's "no," so also Jesus' "yes" reversed Adam's "no."

Where was Mary?

During his ministry, Jesus seems to have chosen an "inner circle" of disciples: Peter, James, and John. I've always thought of these three as his closest followers, and maybe they were, but they were not his star pupils. Peter was the one whose faith failed when he tried to walk on water. He was the one who rambled on about building tabernacles when he saw the vision of Jesus' Transfiguration. And he was the one who would deny he ever knew Jesus that same night of Jesus' prayer. James and John had argued over who would be ahead of whom in the kingdom. So I sometimes wonder if the "inner circle" was really the remedial class. These were the guys who needed more attention from Jesus because they were slow in "getting it." Of course, they *would* get it; Peter would become the leader of the apostles, and John would go on to write the fourth gospel and the book of Revelation. In any case, when Jesus went deeper into the olive grove to pray, he took Peter, James, and John with him. But as he prayed into the night, they too showed their human weakness and fell asleep.

Somewhere not too far away were the other eight disciples (Judas had already gone off to lead the soldiers to the garden). The rest of them were probably resting, talking, maybe finishing off the last of the wine, and generally just taking a break from the hard days of walking and teaching in the hot sun. But we can imagine another group sitting under the olive trees: not only the eight disciples but also others who had been at the Last Supper with them. There were likely some of the seventy whom Jesus had commissioned to teach in his name. There were probably other disciples, who were not members of the twelve but who nevertheless followed Jesus. Tradition says Mark, the author of the second gospel, was there as a young boy (see Mark 14:51–52). And we can assume that the women were there, too, including Jesus' mother, Mary. She couldn't hear his prayer, or see his agony, but his agony would be hers, too, very soon. Mary must have been very worried that coming into Jerusalem was not going to end well. And she was about to feel very alone in her care for her Son, because the gospel writers tell us that when Jesus was arrested, all the disciples "deserted him and fled." Mary must have been extremely distraught, and probably tried to follow where the soldiers were taking her Son. I imagine it was only because the other disciples took her away for her own safety that she didn't. But she was one of the few people with him when he was on the Cross.

What does it tell us about Jesus?

There came a time in the early Church when the Church Fathers debated about just how unified, and just how distinct, were the two natures of divinity and humanity in Jesus Christ. Some proposed such a unity that it seemed as though they were saying the humanity of Jesus was swallowed up in the divinity like a drop of oil in the ocean. Others wanted to emphasize how the divinity in him could never be changed, so they proposed a kind of union in which the two natures were really kept separate—but that made it sound as if Jesus had multiple personalities! Still others tried to compromise by saying that the divine Word of God became the mind of Jesus, in effect, "replacing" the human mind. They said this because they reasoned that only if Jesus *didn't* have a human mind would it be possible for him to completely avoid sin. Furthermore, folks such as these argued that for Jesus Christ to be truly one person (and not two) he could only have one mind, and one will; otherwise he would argue with himself.

When the dust settled on these debates, the Church concluded that for Jesus Christ to be *both* fully divine and truly human, he must have *both* a divine mind and a human mind. That means he has two wills: the divine will (the same divine will as the Father and the Holy Spirit) and his human will. The Church would come to describe him as *one divine person in two natures*. The one person of Jesus Christ has within him the mind and will of the Trinity, as well as a real human mind and will. So when Jesus prays to the Father, you could also say that the human in him is praying to the divine in him. And when he submits to the will of the Father, you could also say that his human will is deciding to be obedient to the divine will within him, which is the same divine will as the will of the Father and the Holy Spirit.

So Jesus Christ really did (and still does) have two minds, two wills. He must have a human mind and will, or else he wouldn't be a complete human, and he wouldn't really be one of us. But he also has a divine mind and will, and that mind and will is the same mind and will of the Holy Trinity. And yet, Jesus does not have two personalities. He is one person, because of the inseparable union of divinity with humanity, and so there is no conflict within him.

We remember Jesus' agony in the garden on the same night of the year that we remember his Last Supper and celebrate the institution of the Eucharist. This is Holy Thursday, the night before Good Friday. Many parishes reenact the foot washing from the gospel of John. Some churches will hold a Tenebrae service, which commemorates Jesus' agony and arrest in the garden.

What aspects of this mystery should we imitate?

It is probably obvious that we, too, should say to the Father, "not my will, but yours be done." Sometimes this is hard to do. Sometimes it is agony. Sometimes we go kicking and screaming, demanding to have our will, and the Father's will is done anyway. Other times we choose our will over the Father's, and he lets us do that; then we have to deal with the consequences. Since we cannot see the future, we can never really know what's best for us. And even if we could know the best possible future, we would not know how to bring it about. St. John Henry Newman said in his autobiography, *Apologia pro Vita sua*, "God knows what is my greatest happiness, but I do not. . . . Thus God leads us by strange ways. . . . We are blind; left to ourselves we should take the wrong way; we must leave it to him." To surrender our wills to the will of God is sometimes the hardest thing to do. But it is always the best thing to do.

MEDITATION

The Agony in the Garden is the agony of inner conflict. Jesus Christ is unique among humanity in that he has two wills, and yet he knew the perfect obedience of the human will cooperating with the divine.

12.

THE SCOURGING AT THE PILLAR

The Paradox of Impassible Suffering

What is the Scourging at the Pillar?

Read Matthew 27:15–26 (parallels in Mark 15:6–15, Luke 23:16–25, and also mentioned in John 19:1).

The scourging at the pillar, sometimes called the flagellation or flogging, is when Jesus was tied to a pillar and whipped. We often hear of "thirty-nine lashes," but the gospels don't actually say how many lashes Jesus was given. There was a tradition of giving thirty-nine, because the Jewish law set the limit at forty (Dt 25:3), and since you didn't want to miss count and break the law, you stopped at thirty-nine. Another tradition says that a man would die from forty lashes, and so it didn't pay to kill him and make him miss his execution.

But the interesting thing about this story is that Pontius Pilate actually tried to go easy on Jesus. Remember that his wife had warned him to leave Jesus alone, because of a dream she had (Mt 27:19). So Pilate tried to let Jesus off with a warning, but the people wouldn't have it. He tried to send him off to Herod, but that didn't work. And then he tried to let him go as a holiday mercy, but the people called for the freedom of Barabbas instead. So finally he tried to see if torturing him would be enough for the people. But it wasn't: they wanted his death. And Pilate was backed into a corner. He had already made some mistakes with the Jewish people that had gotten him in trouble with the emperor. Another mistake and he could be transferred, and to be removed in disgrace from a post like Judea—well, that couldn't be good for one's career. When the members of the Jerusalem council tell Pilate, "If you release him, you are not a Friend of Caesar" (Jn 19:12), this is a direct threat that they will go to the emperor and complain about him if he doesn't do what they demand.

Incidentally, there was an early tradition that Pilate himself later converted to Christianity. If so, his conversion probably came after he was finally removed from office and sent back to Rome in disgrace. There is also a tradition that Pilate's wife (the legend says her name was Claudia) converted to Christianity and joined the Church in Jerusalem.

And so Jesus was whipped. He submitted to a mockery of justice, and then submitted to the lash. The Word became flesh, and dwelt among us: he came into the world he created, and then let the world take out its anger on him.

In Rome, in the church of Santa Prassede, there is a small pillar that is said to be the very pillar that Jesus was tied to when he was whipped. It's not the kind of pillar that holds up a building, but the kind you would tie your donkey to. It is reasonable to believe that the first followers of Jesus remembered that pillar, and showed it to their converts. And since Christians have been living in Jerusalem ever since, it is also reasonable to believe that fathers pointed out that pillar to their sons, and mothers to their daughters, down through the generations, until the empire recognized the Christian faith, and the pillar was brought to Rome.

Where was Mary?

When Jesus was arrested, we are told that all the disciples fled, and presumably, they took Mary with them. But it's probably safe to assume that at every point in the events that followed she was as close to Jesus as she could be. No doubt when the crowd shouted for the release of Barabbas, she was there. Maybe she even had a moment of hope when Pilate offered to release Jesus. And when they shouted for Jesus' crucifixion, she was there, her heart breaking.

We don't know if Mary witnessed the scourging at the pillar. It is possible, since punishments such as flogging were done in public in order to be a deterrent to onlookers. And if the pillar he was tied to was used to tie up animals, then it would be along the street, out in the open. Thinking about what it must have felt like for Mary to witness the scourging of her Son should help us to remember that Jesus was not only executed; he was tortured first. The fear of so many people, and their refusal to repent, fermented into anger and hatred, and then was expressed in unbridled cruelty as the world took out its anger on the one person who could save it.

What does it tell us about Jesus?

Philosophers (and the Church Fathers) tell us that divinity cannot suffer, because suffering is a lack of something—to suffer is to need—and God does not lack or need anything. And so, since Jesus is God in the flesh, his divine nature cannot suffer. The theological word for this is *impassibility*. And yet, the Church Fathers tell us that in him, "the impassible suffered." How is that possible?

Well, the simplest answer is that we have to remember that the Incarnation means that the Logos, the second person of the Trinity, has two natures. Christ is divine, but he is also human. And so in reality, only his human nature suffered; his divine nature did not. But that's not the whole story, because those two natures are united in one person. Jesus is, after all, only one person, so anything he experiences in his human body is experienced by his whole person.

The Church Fathers wrote about a concept called (in Latin) the *communicatio idiomatum* or "communication of idioms." Idioms are particular properties that are unique to each of Jesus' two natures. For example, the property of weakness and susceptibility to pain and death is a property that is unique to Christ's human nature. So although it was only the Son (in his human nature) who suffered the Passion, the Father and the Holy Spirit also know what it means to suffer. God is not subjected to suffering, as we are, and most important, God is not helpless in the face of suffering. In fact, it is because God is not susceptible to suffering that God can overcome our suffering and heal us. If we experience sickness, we need a physician, not a fellow patient. God is that physician: one who knows our pain but can also do something about it.

What aspects of this mystery should we imitate?

Jesus did not deserve the punishment of the scourging at the pillar. And yet he did not complain. How many times do we complain, even when we are suffering the consequences of our own choices? Can we follow Jesus' example, and accept the trials of this world without complaining? And can we follow Mary's example, and try to stay as close to Jesus at all times?

MEDITATION

The divine and eternal Word of God came to live the life of a human being, and was even willing to submit to the brutality of the very ones he came to save. He let the world take out its hatred on him, and he still wanted to save it. The one who could not suffer voluntarily submitted to suffering so that those who could not escape their suffering could know peace.

13.

THE CROWNING WITH THORNS

The Paradox of the Subjected King

What is the Crowning with Thorns?

Read Matthew 27:27–31 (parallel in Mark 15:16–20).

If Pilate was trying to let Jesus live, his soldiers were not so civilized. They seem to have taken every opportunity to make Jesus' ordeal the most humiliating and dehumanizing it could be. There's no way to know if these soldiers hated Jesus for who he was, or if they just hated all Jews. Or maybe they just treated every prisoner this way. But they stripped him naked (possibly the most humiliating part of the whole thing for a Jewish man) and dressed Jesus up like a pantomime king. With a reed for a scepter, they twisted up a wreath of thorns and pressed it down onto his head, ripping into his skin down to the bone. They mocked him, they spat on him, and they beat him. And they were just getting started.

The crown of thorns represents much more than mockery and torture, though. It represents the paradox that the King of the Universe was treated like a village idiot. The Word of God became human, only to end up being dehumanized by the very people he came to save. With the crown of thorns, the world added insult to injury, mockery to hate. In the scourging at the pillar, Jesus took all the hate and resentment that the world had to throw at him.

But as if that wasn't enough, in the crown of thorns, he took on the world's cynicism, derision, and sarcasm.

Where was Mary?

The gospels tell us that after Jesus was mocked and tortured in this way, "they led him out" to be crucified. That implies that he was inside somewhere, probably in the barracks or stables of the Praetorium (Herod's old palace, now being used by Pilate as a headquarters for the Roman legionaries in Jerusalem). The soldiers were probably not really supposed to treat even a condemned criminal this way, and therefore it's unlikely that all of this happened in sight of anyone other than the soldiers themselves. If that causes you to ask, "Then how did the gospel writers know about it, to write it down?" remember that we have reason to believe that at least one of these soldiers would come to follow Christ. Tradition names him as St. Longinus, and he was (according to legend) the soldier who pierced Christ's side with a lance. Not long after that, he would proclaim, "Truly this man was the Son of God!" (Mk 15:39).

In any case, Mary probably did not witness the crowning with thorns for herself, but she certainly would have seen the thorny crown on his head as she followed him on the way to Golgotha. It must have broken her heart to see her boy beaten, his hair wet with blood, the wounds from the thorns bleeding profusely.

What does it tell us about Jesus?

Jesus' parable of the wicked tenants (Mt 21:33–46; Mk 12:1–12; Lk 20:9–19) is a story about a landowner who leased out his vineyard to tenants. When the landowner sent servants to collect the rent, the tenants beat the servants. When the landowner sent his son, they killed him. This parable is an obvious analogy for what

Jesus knew would happen to him. The landowner represents God. The vineyard represents the land of Israel, and all the blessings of being the people of God. The tenants represent the people of the original covenant. The landowner's servants represent the prophets, whom the people mistreated when they gave prophecies that people didn't want to hear. And of course, the landowner's son represents Jesus. It was in this context that Jesus predicted the fall of Jerusalem and the opening up of the possibility of a relationship with God to the Gentiles, in the new covenant.

It is a mystery why it had to be this way. But the Passion, Death, and Resurrection of Jesus was not God's "plan B." Although there was some debate in the Middle Ages over whether Jesus would have had to come if Adam and Eve had not sinned, the question is purely hypothetical. God did not respond to the sin of Adam and Eve by saying, "Wow, I didn't see that coming! What should I do now?" And God did not respond to the rejection of Jesus with some kind of surprised anger as though the salvation of the Gentiles depended on the fall of the Jews and their holy city. And yet, these things happened, and they did lead to the possibility of salvation for all of humanity.

The plans of God are mysterious and filled with paradoxes that we can't quite understand. Here, at the moment of the crowning with thorns, we see a king—the King of kings—voluntarily accepting absolute humiliation so that he could save the very people who had made themselves his enemies. But let us be clear: the eternal providence of God means that we are not just talking about the Jews. The Jews did not kill Jesus. We all killed Jesus. Adam and Eve killed Jesus. You did, and I did. Every human sin, every single sin that you and I have committed, is a thorn digging into the flesh of Christ. And yet he willingly, and lovingly, gives his flesh to save us from our sins. And he continues to offer us his flesh and blood in the Eucharist, so that we can continually remain in him, as he urged us to do (Jn 15:1–10).

What aspects of this mystery should we imitate?

Our enemies, such as they are, are thorns. We have an expression, "thorn in my side," which comes from something St. Paul said in 2 Corinthians, chapter 12. Maybe sometimes you think someone is a thorn in your backside. Or maybe you don't think you have enemies, but if you think about it, you know of one or two people who annoy you, or who have wronged you. Just as every one of our sins is a thorn in Jesus' crown, so every time someone sins against us, it is a thorn in our crown as well. How should we respond to these thorns? The same way Jesus did. He took the pain and called it a labor of love. He didn't fight back; he didn't even complain. He accepted it, and absorbed it, as part of his ministry of atonement. Can we do something similar? Can we take the annoyances, the wrongs, the sins that others hurt us with, and respond with love, out of a commitment to serving others in Jesus' name, and loving our neighbors as he told us to? At the very least, we must let go of wrongs done to us (see 1 Corinthians 13:5–6). It may be hard, but if we think about it, forgiving is actually the best thing for *us*, because holding on to anger only hurts us. Dwelling on the ways in which others have wronged us only clouds our minds with negativity.

To imitate Jesus is to respond to the thorns of life with love. St. Peter, paraphrasing something he heard Jesus say, wrote, "Do not return evil for evil, or insult for insult; but on the contrary, a blessing" (1 Pt 3:9, and see Matthew 5:21–26, 38–48). Many years later, Bishop Fulton Sheen wrote, "Overcome adversaries, not with resistance, but with love." That's how we win: by loving the ones who wrong us. It ends the drama and they don't know what to do with us, except hopefully to reconcile with us—and each time that happens, an enemy becomes a friend. The Roman soldier (St.) Longinus went from being a torturer and mocker of Jesus to one who acknowledged his divinity. The Pharisee (St.) Paul went from being a persecutor of the Church to one of its greatest evangelists. Jesus suffered and died so that the enemies of God (and that includes us) could become not just friends of God but children of God.

MEDITATION

The highest authority in the universe let people belittle him through mockery and sarcasm, because it was through his own complete humiliation that he would raise humanity up out of its debased condition.

14.

THE CARRYING OF THE CROSS

The Paradox of Silent Wisdom

What is the Carrying of the Cross?

Read Luke 23:26–31 (parallels in Matthew 27:32 and Mark 15:21).

Those condemned to die by crucifixion were made to carry their own crosses. Most likely this meant carrying the crossbeam, since the vertical pole was probably already fixed in place at the roadside outside the city gate. Executions were public to make a point, but this particular kind of execution was no spectacle. It was slow; for the onlooker, crucifixions were almost boring. But the condemned person usually took long enough to die that the Romans could be sure a lot of people would pass by and get the message.

The *Via Dolorosa*, or the "way of sorrow" in Latin, was the path the procession walked from the Praetorium to the hill called Calvary, or Golgotha, the "place of the skull." A simple internet search will produce many photographs of the path itself, as well as the destination. Just keep in mind that it looked a lot different two thousand years ago, and the actual site of the Crucifixion is now part of the Church of the Holy Sepulcher. The route is only about a third of a mile, which doesn't sound like a lot to us, but Jesus was so badly beaten and broken that he could not carry the crossbeam all the way. The synoptic gospels (Matthew, Mark, and Luke) make it seem as though he didn't actually carry the cross at all, but we know from the short mention in John's gospel that he did carry it at least part of the way (Jn 19:17). Apparently, however, he could not stay on his feet, so the soldiers became impatient with him and conscripted a bystander, Simon of Cyrene, to carry Jesus' cross. According to the tradition of our Stations of the Cross, Simon *helped* him carry the crossbeam, though Luke says he carried the cross behind Jesus. Perhaps he started out trying to help Jesus but ended up just carrying it himself. Either way, according to the Stations, Jesus still fell two more times even after Simon was compelled to help him.

Simon of Cyrene doesn't appear anywhere else in the Bible, but ancient tradition says that he became a member of the Church after that. It could be that he was already a disciple of Jesus, and that's why he was watching—or following—the procession. Mark tells us that Simon had two sons, Alexander and Rufus, which indicates that the original audience of Mark's gospel in Rome knew who they were (see Mark 15:21, and also Romans 16:13).

Where was Mary?

By this time Mary was probably following the procession as closely as she could. The fourth of the Stations of the Cross, *Jesus Meets His Mother*, describes at least one moment when their eyes met. We are also told that Jesus fell, multiple times. How many times did Mary protect him from falling as a toddler? Now she couldn't stop him from falling. How many times did she pick him up and hold him in her arms? Now she could not, and she would not be able to touch him again until it was time to take him down from the cross. She would hold her Son again only when he was dead.

Luke tells us that there was quite a large crowd following the procession. It had been a large crowd that welcomed Jesus into

Jerusalem as he rode the donkey in his "triumphal entry." Perhaps
many of those people who put their coats down to make a path
for him and waved palm branches were now following this polar
opposite kind of parade. Women were "beating their breasts and
wailing for him." Although this sounds to us like an extreme dis-
play of emotion, it was a typical kind of mourning in that time
and place. But Jesus responded by saying they should not weep
for him: they should weep for themselves, and their children, and
for their holy city Jerusalem. This is why he called them "daughters of Jerusalem," to remind them of the Old Testament book of
Lamentations (see Lamentations, chapter 1). That book mourns
the fall of Jerusalem, and Jesus knew that within a generation,
Jerusalem would fall again.

What does it tell us about Jesus?

In both the fourth gospel and in the book of Revelation, John
refers to Jesus as the *Word* of God. Here the English word *Word* is
a translation of the Greek word *Logos*. But *Logos* doesn't just mean
a spoken word. It has a beautiful range of meaning that includes
concepts such as reason, rationality, and wisdom. In fact, John's
description of Jesus as the *Word* is understood to be a fulfillment
of Old Testament personifications of God's wisdom, in which
the Wisdom of God is the agent of creation (see, for example,
Proverbs 3:13–20). And in the Gospel of John, we read that is it
Christ, the Word, who is the agent of creation: "All things came
to be through him, and without him nothing came to be" (Jn 1:3).
In fact, the Church Fathers pointed out that in Genesis, we read
that God created by his *Word* when he said, "Let there be . . ." And
icons of Mary with Jesus seated on her lap are often referred to
as Mary, *Seat of Wisdom*. So the Son of God is the Word of God
and the Wisdom of God, and *as* God, he is co-Creator with the
Father and the Holy Spirit. And as the Church fathers liked to say,

the One who hung the stars in the heavens was himself hung on a cross for our sake.

There were a lot of other Old Testament prophecies that were fulfilled by Jesus. Some of them were never really thought of as prophecies of the Messiah until after Jesus' life, Death, and Resurrection. One of these is the "Suffering Servant" of Isaiah. Here the prophet says: "We had all gone astray like sheep, all following our own way; But the Lord laid upon him the guilt of us all. Though harshly treated, he submitted, and did not open his mouth; like a lamb led to slaughter, or a sheep silent before shearers, he did not open his mouth" (53:6–7).

Why, at this crucial (literally) moment of Jesus' ministry, did he remain silent? Why was Wisdom incarnate content to say nothing? When Jesus was still small, the prophet Simeon said that he was "destined . . . to be a sign that will be contradicted . . ." (Lk 2:34). It seems he was saying that Jesus himself would be the sign. Or perhaps the Cross was to be the sign. Either way, it was a sign that would be contradicted. At this point, the time for parables and lessons was over. The people had come to their conclusions about Jesus, and the majority rejected him. There was nothing more to say. Jesus himself, his voluntary sacrifice, and his Crucifixion would say everything at this point.

It was wisdom for the Creator of the universe to come into the world as a helpless baby. It was wisdom for the God of love to give his creatures free will, freedom even to reject his love. It was wisdom for the Author of right and truth to bring justice through mercy and offer all those who have rejected him forgiveness and reconciliation. It is wisdom for the Holy One to accept sinners and call them holy. It is wisdom for the Alpha and the Omega to ordain that the first would be last and the last would be first. It is wisdom for the Ancient of Days to make all things new. The wisdom of the world is foolishness to God (see 1 Corinthians 3:19).

And Christ crucified is a stumbling block to Jews and foolishness to Gentiles (see 1 Corinthians 1:23). This is the paradox of God's silent wisdom.

What aspects of this mystery should we imitate?

We all know that Jesus said, "Take up your cross and follow me." He apparently said this on more than one occasion—see Matthew 10:38–39 (parallel in Luke 14:27, 33) and Matthew 16:24–26 (parallels in Mark 8:34–37 and Luke 9:23–25). But we often forget just how strange that must have sounded to the disciples *before* the Crucifixion. And even more surprising, he made this a requirement for discipleship! In context, he said, "Whoever does not take up the cross and follow me is not worthy of me," and "Whoever does not carry the cross and follow me cannot be my disciple." These are strong words, again, especially before he had carried his own cross. He said, "If any want to become my followers, *let them deny themselves*, and take up their cross, and follow me." So to be a follower of Jesus means following him on the *Via Dolorosa*, the way of sorrow, or as it is sometimes translated, the way of suffering.

Jesus never promised that commitment to him would mean protection from suffering. Everyone suffers in this life, some more than others, but that's not the test. Good and bad things happen to both good and bad people. The test is not what happens to us; it's how we handle it. Are our lives characterized by seeking comfort and complaining about it when things don't go our way? Or are our lives characterized by following Christ regardless of the circumstances? For each of us, to carry *our* cross means to lean into it. Whatever our cross is, to carry it means to embrace it, not to fight against it.

Now of course if our cross is illness, we should take advantage of all that medical science has to offer for our healing. If our cross is abuse or injustice, I'm not advocating suffering in silence. Jesus suffered in silence, but although he was innocent, his suffering was voluntary. At other times, abuses and injustices need to be confronted and opposed. Yet, in our suffering we have to be honest with ourselves and admit that sometimes our suffering is the consequence of our own sin, and sometimes the wisest thing we can say is nothing at all. Jesus followed through with his mission, regardless of the personal sacrifice. Mary followed Jesus as closely as she could, no matter how much it made her suffer. If we want to follow Jesus, and follow the example of Mary, we will do what's right in any given moment, regardless of the consequences. We will deny ourselves, admit "it's not all about me," and lean into the cross of self-sacrifice. In many ways, this life on earth is a "way of suffering." If anyone tells us that prosperity and happiness is our divine right, they are selling us "another gospel" (Gal 1:8). But as we carry our crosses faithfully in this life, we know that eternal life with Jesus will be our inheritance. And while we're at it, let's try to do it without complaining.

MEDITATION

The innocent one accepted the injustice of false accusations and charges without complaining or protesting, so that we who are guilty could be acquitted of our sins.

15.

THE CRUCIFIXION
The Paradox of a Dying God

What is the Crucifixion?

The account of the Crucifixion of Jesus is, of course, in all four gospels. Each account is a little different; each one gives us a different perspective and some different (but overlapping) information. Many books have been written about the Crucifixion of Jesus, as well as about how to harmonize the accounts. For our meditation, the details are not as important as the overall impression. The Crucifixion is found in Matthew 27:33–56, Mark 15:22–41, Luke 23:33–49, and John 19:16–37. I don't recommend that you read all four accounts back to back; it will just be overwhelming. However, you should read them all eventually.

Crucifixion was one of many methods of execution used by the Romans. It was the slowest and most humiliating method. You know how our crucifixes show Jesus wrapped at his waist with a loin cloth? In reality the person being crucified was completely naked, exposed to the extreme heat and sun as well as to public shame. Sometimes it took days for a person to die. Victims of crucifixion suffocated slowly as muscles tired from having to lift the weight of the torso just to catch a breath. Most were tied to the crossbeam, but when the Romans wanted to be especially cruel, the soldiers drove large iron nails through the person's hands and feet. As we have seen, they did want to be especially cruel to Jesus, but he was probably tied as well as nailed, so the nails would not have to hold him on the cross. They were there purely to add more pain and suffering.

Since crucifixion was arguably the worst way to die, and since the Romans considered themselves civilized, the cross was reserved for the worst criminals of the lowest social classes. By law a Roman citizen could not be crucified. This is why a little more than thirty years later, the apostle Paul would be beheaded: a quick and painless death for a Roman citizen. But St. Peter would follow his Lord to the cross, just as Jesus said he would (see John 21:18–19). Except that when Peter protested that he did not deserve to die in the same way Jesus did, the soldiers at that time mocked him, too, and crucified him upside down.

Many other followers of Jesus would be crucified, beginning with the persecution of the emperor Nero in Rome in the mid-sixties, and then during wave after wave of persecution for the next two and a half centuries. Christians died at the hands of the Romans until the emperor Constantine legalized Christianity in the year AD 313. He eventually outlawed crucifixion as a means of execution.

Still, Jesus' crucifixion was unique, because he was without sin, and his death was a sacrifice for the rest of humanity. Ironically, his Cross became the symbol to be opposed (Lk 2:34), the emblem of victory over sin and death, and the sign of freedom in Christ.

Where was Mary?

Mary was, at all times, as close to Jesus as she could be both spiritually and literally. This is one reason why Mary is a supreme example for us to follow. The gospels tell us that—except for the women, and the youngest of the twelve, John—all of the remaining disciples had run away, or were hiding and watching from a distance. Even John's older brother James was nowhere to be found, but their mother was there, along with Mary Magdalene, and Jesus' aunt, whose name was also Mary. (It was a very popular name because in Hebrew, Miriam is the name of Moses's sister.) Perhaps the women were braver than the men because they felt they had less to lose in a culture where they didn't have concerns for careers or upward mobility. Perhaps John was bolder than the other men out of sheer youthful enthusiasm and innocence. It's worth noting that of the four evangelists, only John was an eye-witness to the Crucifixion.

It's also important to remember that Jesus could see who was there. He could see those who were willing to risk their own safety to stick by him. Jesus saw his mother and the other women, and he saw John. He told his mother Mary that from that moment forward, John would be a son to her. And he told John that from that time on, Mary would be a mother to him. This reveals two things to us. First, it confirms that Mary had no other children of her own, not even after Jesus, because if she had any other children, they would have been responsible to care for her, not John. Second, the Church teaches that John represents all of us in the Church, as he accepts Mary as his mother. Just as Mary became the mother of Jesus' disciple John, she also became the mother of all of Jesus' disciples; she is the Mother of the Church.

In the book of Revelation, Mary is depicted as the woman crowned with twelve stars, which symbolizes that she is a daughter of the twelve tribes of Israel (see Revelation 12). In John's vision, written down a little more than sixty years after the Crucifixion, he saw the woman (Mary) give birth to a man (Jesus). A dragon tried to kill the man (as Herod the Great had tried to kill the infant Jesus), but the dragon's plan failed. Then the text of Revelation says that "the dragon became angry with the woman and went off to wage war against *the rest of her offspring,* those who keep God's commandments, and bear witness to Jesus" (Rv 12:17, italics added). The rest of her children: that's the Church; that's us. And the persecution of the early Christians was seen by John as ultimately being the work of the same dragon who tried to kill Jesus: that is, Satan. The point is that all Christians are the "other children" of Mary. She is our mother.

And so Mary saw her Son die a slow, agonizing death. She knew his death had a purpose, but that can't have made it much easier on her. The Crucifixion and Death of Jesus is, of course, one of the traditional seven sorrows of Mary: the seven swords said to pierce Mary's heart, according to the prophecy of Simeon. I sometimes wonder if the angel Gabriel said anything to Mary at the annunciation, like, "Full disclosure, if you say yes to this you're going to have to give him up: you're going to have to watch him die; you're going to have to bury your Son. No parent should ever have to bury a child, but you will. The good news is, in giving up your only child, you will become a Mother to everyone who will call him their brother. But knowing that won't make it any easier. And yet, if you trust God with this, it will mean the salvation of the world."

There is a beautiful painting by the Renaissance artist Raphael. It's titled *Madonna della Seggiola*, but more commonly known as the "Madonna of the Chair," and it depicts a young Mary, seated (in a chair, as you might have guessed), holding a chubby baby Jesus on her lap. Jesus is snuggled into Mary's embrace, and a toddler, John the Baptist, looks on. But Mary is looking right at *you*, the viewer. And she has this look in her eyes, as if she's saying, "You can't have him yet. He's mine for now. I will give him up when the time comes, and *your* sin will put him on the Cross— so no, you can't have him yet." That may not be how we tend to think of Mary, and of course she wouldn't really be that focused on herself. Still, I wonder what history's only other sinless human being was thinking about *us* when she watched her Son die. No doubt she had mixed emotions, and no doubt those emotions included compassion for those who would call her Mother. But when we pray for Mary's intercession, let us never forget to pray with the humility that comes from the knowledge that *we* put her Son on that cross.

What does it tell us about Jesus?

And so the divine Word of God, who had become human, had now died. But how can we say that Divinity died? Surely God cannot die, can he? Well, we *can* say that God died because Jesus Christ is fully God, and Jesus Christ died. But even though that is correct, we also know that it was really just Christ's *human nature* that died.

In fact, the two natures of divinity and humanity in Jesus are so unified that it is precisely the union of his two natures that is the very nexus, the link, of the connection between God and all humanity. Think of it like a chain. At one end of the chain is God, the Trinity. God's divinity is the same divinity as the divine nature of Jesus, so the divine nature of the Trinity *is* the divine nature of Jesus Christ. At the other end of the chain is humanity. We are all connected to one another through our common human nature, and in this sense, we are connected to Jesus, too, because he shares that same human nature. So the union between the divine nature and the human nature in Jesus—we call this the *hypostatic union*, which means the *personal* union—that union is the very link that connects divinity to humanity, and makes it possible for humanity to be reconciled to God.

Salvation is reconciliation with God. It is the reunion of God and humanity, who were estranged by sin. And that reunion is made possible by the *hypostatic* union, the unity of divinity and humanity in Jesus Christ. Divinity and humanity are brought together *by* him because they are unified *in* him. Our only hope of salvation is in the person of Jesus Christ. Jesus died to make it possible for all of humanity to be saved, even his murderers. From the Cross, while he was dying, he was interceding for humanity, saying, "Father, forgive them."

He also said something that sounds strange on the surface. He said, "My God, my God, why have you forsaken me?" But did God the Father forsake Jesus? There is a sense in which the Father had to "turn his back" on Jesus, in order for Jesus to be the sacrifice for all human sin, and in order not to intervene and call the whole thing off. But it's important to know that when Jesus said that, he was actually quoting Psalm 22. Back then, documents often didn't have titles the way we think of titles. The "title" of a document was the first line. So this psalm wasn't known as "Psalm 22" to the people of Jesus' day. It was known as the *My God, my God, why have you forsaken me?* psalm. When Jesus quoted its opening line, he was reminding all who were there to hear that the psalm starts out as a psalm of despair—it looks really bad right now—but ends up as a psalm of hope. Anyone who knew that psalm, and who heard Jesus quote it, would have known that the real theme of that psalm is *Those who put their trust in the Lord will not be disappointed* (see verses 3–5). Notice that Psalm 22 also turns out to be a prophecy of the Crucifixion:

> All who see me mock me;
>> they curl their lips and jeer;
>> they shake their heads at me:
> "He relied on the LORD—let him deliver him;
>> if he loves him, let him rescue him." . . .
> Like water my life drains away;
>> all my bones are disjointed.
> My heart has become like wax,
>> it melts away within me.
> As dry as a potsherd is my throat;
>> my tongue cleaves to my palate;
>> you lay me in the dust of death.
> Dogs surround me;

> a pack of evildoers closes in on me.
> They have pierced my hands and my feet
> I can count all my bones.
> They stare at me and gloat;
>> they divide my garments among them;
>> for my clothing they cast lots. (vv. 8–9, 15–19)

But then the psalm ends:

> All the ends of the earth
>> will remember and turn to the LORD;
> All the families of nations
>> will bow low before him.
> For kingship belongs to the LORD,
>> the ruler over the nations.
> All who sleep in the earth
>> will bow low before God;
> All who have gone down into the dust
>> will kneel in homage.
> And I will live for the LORD;
>> my descendants will serve you.
> The generation to come will be told of the Lord,
>> that they may proclaim to a people yet unborn
>> the deliverance you have brought. (vv. 28–32)

And that is Jesus' message, his homily from the Cross! Even as he was dying there, even as people kept on mocking him, he forgave them all—and not just those who were there at that time but also all people of all times whose sin put him there. It took him six hours to die. He was crucified at nine o'clock in the morning. At noon the sky became dark, and at three o'clock he died. At that moment, the curtain that closed off the holiest sanctuary in the Temple was torn from top to bottom. This was an act of God that signified that Jesus' death had opened up access to God to everyone.

What aspects of this mystery should we imitate?

All the gospel writers tell us that Jesus was one of at least three men crucified that day. Matthew and Mark tell us that there were thieves who were crucified with Jesus, who also mocked him. But Luke tells us that one of those being crucified, whom tradition names as Dismas, apparently recognized Jesus and knew who he was, since he acknowledged that Jesus was innocent. Further, he turned to Jesus, called him by name, and asked, "Remember me when you come into your kingdom." Jesus responded by saying, "Truly I tell you, today you will be with me in paradise."

I want to suggest that we should be like the "Good Thief." First, we have to admit that we are "thieves" whose sins merit punishment, but who have been acquitted of all crimes by the mercy of the Judge of the universe. And then, we have to put our trust in Jesus for our salvation. It's so easy to believe the message of the world, that people are okay just the way they are, and that we each deserve everything we can get. It's harder and more humbling to admit that we do not really deserve anything other than punishment, and if we have any blessings at all (let alone salvation) it is only by the mercy of Jesus. So we put our trust in Jesus, because those who put their trust in the Lord will not be disappointed.

MEDITATION

The only one in the universe who cannot die willingly accepted death so that we who do not deserve eternal life could have it anyway.

PART 4

The Glorious Mysteries (Wednesdays and Sundays)

A Mystery in History: The Rosary Protects a Woman from a Serial Killer

Ted Bundy is one of the most famous serial killers in American history. In 1978, he attacked young women in a small sorority house in Florida. One woman in the house who was not attacked shared with a priest that she was praying the Rosary in bed that night.

Many people believe death passed over this young woman because of the rosary she held. Mother Mary protected her. The Church Fathers had a saying: "Where the Sign of the Cross is, evil is weakest." When that cross is a crucifix, and that crucifix is attached to a rosary, evil is not only weak: it is afraid.

16.

THE RESURRECTION
The Paradox of the Resurrection Body

What is the Resurrection?

Read John 20:1–29 (the Resurrection is also found in Matthew 28:1–10, Mark 16:1–8, and Luke 24:1–12, 36–49).

Just as the prophets Elijah and Elisha had done in their time, Jesus had "raised" several people from death during his ministry, including his friend Lazarus. The ability to bring back life from death demonstrates a power that can only come from God. But all of those people would die again. Technically, what they experienced was not resurrection but resuscitation. Resurrection, by contrast, is the ultimate raising to life eternal. Resurrection does not allow for a person to die again, because resurrection is the fulfillment of God's plan for the human being.

Resurrection is the reunion of a person's spirit (or soul) with his or her glorified body. Death separates the spirit from the body, but this separation is only temporary. For Jesus, that separation only lasted about a day and a half. I know we are used to saying that he was dead for three days, but actually he was raised "on the third day," so the body of Jesus was actually dead from Friday afternoon until early Sunday morning, about a day and half. But the fact that Jesus didn't stay dead is only the beginning of the good news for us. The rest of the story is that Jesus' Resurrection becomes the prototype for our own. The fact that he overcame death in resurrection makes

our own resurrection possible. Although our spirits may be separated from our bodies for a much longer time than a day and a half,
eventually our bodies will be raised to be rejoined with our spirits,
so that we can once again be whole, redeemed, and glorified—ready
for eternal life in the kingdom.

But what is good news for us was bad news for the enemies of
Jesus and his disciples. Not only were they unwilling to believe in
the resurrection, but also they sure didn't want the story being told.
As soon as Jesus was dead, the Temple council convinced Pontius
Pilate to post a guard so no one could steal his body (Mt 27:62–68).
They knew that there had been predictions that Jesus would rise
from the dead, and they reasoned that someone might try to move
the body and claim that he was alive. The soldiers who stood guard
would later have to be bribed to make up a story about disciples
stealing the body of Jesus (see Matthew 28:11–15). And as Matthew
tells us, that story was still being told at the time he wrote his gospel.
Those who did not believe that Jesus was in fact exactly who he said
he was found it easier to believe that the disciples had stolen the
body and lied about it. Perhaps that *is* easier to believe, but then faith
has never been about believing what is easiest or most convenient.
There have been a lot of theories over the centuries about what
"really" happened to Jesus, or to his body. He was knocked out, and
later "came to." He was in a coma, and later woke up. He died, but
someone else who looked like him took his place. Or he never really
hung on a cross at all. But as St. Paul says, "If Christ has not been
raised, your faith is vain; you are still in your sins" (1 Cor 15:17).

Where was Mary?

Jesus' Mother was there with him on the Via Dolorosa. She was
there with him at Golgotha. She was there as he was taken down
from the Cross (at least we assume so, as did Michelangelo when
he created his finest masterpiece, the *Pietà*). The gospels don't

specifically say that she was there when Jesus was laid in the tomb, but it seems reasonable to assume that Mary was among the "women who had come from Galilee with him" (Lk 23:55–56) who prepared his body for burial. It's also not clear whether she was with the women who went to the tomb that Sunday morning. It is hard to think of a reason why she wouldn't be, but equally hard to think of a reason why the gospel writers wouldn't specifically include her in the story if she had been there.

In any case, it turns out the women were the first evangelists of Christ's Resurrection; they were the first to see the empty tomb and tell others about it. The men didn't believe their story, but the women were the first ones to see the risen Lord. At the very least, Mary must have been in that upper room when Jesus appeared to the disciples there and said, "Peace be with you." Very few of us can even imagine what she must have felt. Only a mother who has lost a child, and received that child back again, can begin to relate. All of the sorrow that the prophet Simeon had predicted was now gone. All of the suffering was over—for her Son, that is. But the suffering of her "other children," the Church, was just beginning.

One final thought about Mary and the resurrection. Remember that Mary was assumed into heaven, body and soul. According to tradition, her assumption took place three days after her death, though this part of the story was certainly meant to mirror her Son's experience. The point is that Mary experienced the reunion of her body and spirit virtually immediately after her death. She did not have to go through purgatory, and she does not have to wait for the Second Coming of Jesus to experience the resurrection. Her assumption *was* her resurrection. And so she is already experiencing eternal life in her spiritual body, and she is the only one (other than Jesus) who already exists in the heavenly realm with her body.

What does it tell us about Jesus?

The Resurrection of Jesus raises a lot of questions. Why couldn't some people recognize him right away, but others apparently did? Why did he tell Mary Magdalene not to cling to him in John's gospel but allow the women to cling to him in Matthew's? And why did he tell Mary Magdalene not to touch him when he told Thomas to put his finger *into* the nail holes in his hands and his hand *into* his side? And how can he walk through the walls of a locked room, if he still needs to eat breakfast? Well, don't get your hopes up for me to answer all these questions, but I can point to the one overarching paradox that encompasses them all—that is, the resurrection body.

St. Paul calls it the "spiritual body" (1 Cor 15), which sounds like a contradiction. But remember that the spiritual and the physical are not at odds in the Christian worldview. At our death, the physical part of ourselves will be separated from the spiritual, so that each can be purified of the corruption of sin. The body is purified by burial, and the spirit is purified by purgatory. But at the resurrection, both are raised and reunited. The newly reconstituted whole person—a spiritual body, or a spirit in a resurrection body—is prepared for eternity in the spiritual realm. The resurrected body is the same body we have now, but it will be transformed and glorified.

The resurrection body of Jesus was both physical and spiritual. It was the same human body that hung on the Cross, but it was glorified. On one hand, the fact that the same body he had in life was raised made him recognizable. But on the other, the fact that his body was glorified (or that his divine glory was unveiled in it) made him hard to recognize for some people. The fact that Jesus had a physical body and was not a ghost meant that he was tangible. But the fact that his body was now suited to the spiritual realm meant that he could not stay on earth indefinitely. Those who loved him could not cling to him; they would have to let him go again, not to death but to ultimate life. The fact that Jesus was raised bodily meant that he could eat, but the fact that his body was a spiritual body meant that he now existed outside of normal space and time, so he could apparently walk through walls. I don't mean this to be an attempt to satisfactorily answer all the questions. But just as it would never be enough to say that Jesus is only divine *or* only human (we must say that he is both), it is also true that it would never be enough to say that his resurrection was *only* physical (that would be resuscitation) or *only* spiritual (as if it were simply a metaphor for "going to heaven"). No, we must say that the resurrection body is *both* material *and* spiritual.

There were those in the early centuries of the Church, however, who tried to say that Jesus was only divine or only human. Interestingly, both of these extremes ended up denying the physicality of the Resurrection. Those who claimed Christ was human only, and not divine, said that his Resurrection was a metaphor for eternal life. Those who claimed that he was divine only, and not human, didn't believe he ever had a real human body in the first place. Both groups denied the resurrection of the body. That is why it was so important for the gospel writers to emphasize that Jesus was tangible, and that he could eat: because his body, not just his spirit, was raised from the dead.

What aspects of this mystery should we imitate?

The fact that resurrection is *the resurrection of the body*, as we say in the Apostles' Creed, means that we are not just spirits, who hope to transcend the body and discard it. We are embodied spirits, who hope for the redemption of our whole being, spirit and body. This means that the body is an essential part of who we are. To be redeemed without the body would be to be only partially redeemed. Therefore, we must respect our bodies as one of our greatest gifts from God. Any time we disrespect creation, we disrespect the Creator, but when we disrespect our own bodies we are opposing the very identity of who God made us to be. So to anticipate our own resurrection, and to demonstrate our faith in God, who raises bodies, we need to take good care of our bodies. We might add something to our weekly rhythm that will help us get in shape and/or stay in shape. Figure out what it would mean to take "healthy" to the next level in our lives. Care for our bodies, and for the bodies of those we love. Resist the temptation to treat our bodies or the bodies of others as objects of entertainment. Reject the social permissions that say there is nothing wrong with abusing and indulging the body. And finally, oppose those cultural trends that treat the body after death as though it's something to be disposed of. And although the Church now allows cremation, we should not scatter ashes, because that is doing the opposite of what God will do in the resurrection.[2]

MEDITATION

The thing that humans most fear, death, is no threat to us because those who die in Christ will rise with Christ. The resurrection of the body means that we are to be raised and redeemed whole, eventually with our bodies and our spirits reunited.

17.

THE ASCENSION
The Paradox of Glorified Humanity

What is the Ascension?

Read Acts 1:1–12 (Luke also summarized the event in Luke 24:50–53).

The Ascension took place forty days after the Resurrection and is the moment when Jesus left his earthly life and ministry and went back to the heavenly realm. It is when he went to be "seated at the right hand" of the Father, as we say in the creeds. We need to be careful, though, that we don't put too much literal stock in the spatial directions here. While it's true that Luke tells us, in both his gospel and in the book of Acts, that Jesus went up and disappeared from everyone's sight, we know that to say heaven is "up" or "above" is a bit too simple. It is not so much "up" as it is another dimension outside of our space and time. And it is not so much "above" us directionally as it is transcendent, a "higher" realm but not one you can get to in a rocket ship. The same goes for the idea of the Son seated at the right hand of the Father. This is metaphorical language. Being at the Father's "right hand" is like saying he is the Father's "right hand man." It means that what the Father does, the Father does through the Son's agency, and the power that the Son wields, he wields by the authority of the Father. It implies an equality of the Son with the Father.

Jesus had told the disciples that he would have to leave them so that the Holy Spirit could come to them and guide them into the next phase of God's plan for salvation: the age of the Church. This does not mean that Jesus and the Holy Spirit can't be in the same place at the same time. And it certainly does not mean that Jesus somehow *became* the Holy Spirit. Jesus and the Holy Spirit are not like Clark Kent and Superman, Peter Parker and Spiderman, or Diana Prince and Wonder Woman. This is not some secret identity thing, or some kind of dis-incarnation. In fact, Jesus and the Holy Spirit have been together the whole time. But it seems that for the followers of Jesus to be filled with the Holy Spirit, it was best for Jesus himself to go (Jn 16:7). They would not see him anymore, but they would have his Spirit.

I think the reason Jesus had to leave the disciples before he could send the Spirit was that as long as he was physically present in the world, his very person was the presence of God on earth. He was, in a very real way, the temple of God, and the presence of God was focused in him, just as it had once been focused in the Jerusalem Temple. But his plan for the gift of the Spirit was that the presence of God was going to be given to all in whom the Spirit would dwell. As St. Paul would later say, the bodies of all Christians are temples of the Holy Spirit (see 1 Corinthians 6:19). The indwelling Holy Spirit would be the presence of God in each of us. As long as Jesus was physically present, the Holy Spirit could work *on* people and *among* people. But after Jesus had gone, the Holy Spirit would live in Jesus' followers and work *in* them and *through* them.

Where was Mary?

As with all of these events, if we are not specifically told that Mary *wasn't* there, then we should probably assume that she was. In this case, we also get a clue from Acts 1:13–14, which affirms that Jesus' Mother was still among the disciples around this time. Although Mary would have been overjoyed to see her Son raised, just forty days later she had to say goodbye to him, not to see him again until her own death and assumption. The ten days between the Ascension and Pentecost must have been an unsettling and confusing time for all of them. They knew what they had seen, but they didn't exactly know what was next. But Mary, who had given Jesus his humanity, had now seen him take it with him to the Father. He had exalted human nature by taking it on in the first place, by raising it from death, and now also by lifting it into heaven. It would be amazing enough that God came down to our level. But now, he was raising us up to his.

What does it tell us about Jesus?

It is very important to make it clear that Jesus did not give up his humanity at the Ascension. Just as the Resurrection was a bodily resurrection, this was bodily ascension. We know that at the annunciation (that is, at his conception in the womb of Mary) the eternal Word of God acquired a human nature and came to exist as a human being. But this did not end at the Ascension. The Son of God's humanity was not temporary. He did not shed his humanity to return to the Father; rather, he brought his humanity with him into the heavenly realm. He is seated at the right hand of the Father in both of his natures, his divinity and his humanity.

By taking on a human nature, he didn't just redeem humanity; he glorified humanity. About one hundred and fifty years later, the great Church Father and bishop Irenaeus of Lyons would write, "The Word of God, our Lord Jesus Christ, through his transcendent love, became what we are, so that he might bring us to become what he is" (*Against Heresies,* Prologue to Book V). In other words: *he became like us, so we could become like him.*

This is more than just a statement about morality. It's not simply saying that he became human so we could become better humans (although that's part of it). But it means that Jesus became human so that we could, as St. Peter wrote, "share in the divine nature" (2 Pt 1:4). That doesn't mean we become gods, of course, but it does mean we become godly, in the way that we were always meant to be before sin entered the equation. It's a concept called *deification*, or in Greek, *theosis*, and it implies that the ultimate goal of the process of sanctification (spiritual growth) is our glorification in the kingdom.

St. Paul also wrote about this, in 2 Corinthians 8:9 (*he became poor so that we could become rich*), and Galatians 3:13–14 (he took on our curse, so that we could have his blessing). This is sometimes referred to as the "wonderful exchange." Jesus came to offer salvation to humanity; that is true, but it's not the whole story. Salvation only makes it possible for humanity to get back to what it was meant to be before the fall. And that's great, of course. By sacrificing his life on the Cross, Jesus reversed the fall of Adam (see 1 Corinthians 15:21–22). But in the Resurrection and Ascension, Jesus took it further: he didn't just restore humanity to what it once was; he lifted human nature higher than it ever was, and brought it into the presence of the Father.

What aspects of this mystery should we imitate?

With the goal of *deification* in mind, we can all take our spiritual growth more seriously. When we read that Jesus said, "Be perfect, therefore, as your heavenly Father is perfect" (Mt 5:48, NRSV), or when we read that Peter wrote, "As he who called you is holy, be holy yourselves in all your conduct; for it is written, 'You shall be holy, for I am holy'" (1 Pt 1:15–16, NRSV), it's important not to simply shrug it off as an exaggeration that no one can live up to. Rather, we must ask ourselves how we can cooperate with Jesus' desire for us to be lifted up to godliness. We must ask: What can I do to "raise up" the level of my spiritual life now, in anticipation of my own ascension?

MEDITATION

Jesus came down to take on a human nature so that he could then raise up human nature to be in union with the divine.

18

PENTECOST

The Paradox of Bold Cowards

What is Pentecost?

Read Acts 2:1–13.

Pentecost was originally a Jewish harvest festival called the Feast of Weeks. The word "Pentecost" is from the Greek, which means the "fiftieth day," since it was celebrated fifty days after the first Sabbath after Passover. It was on the day of the feast of Pentecost that the Holy Spirit came to the apostles. For forty days after the Resurrection, Jesus had stayed around teaching and commissioning his apostles. Then ten days after the Ascension, he kept his promise to fill them with the Holy Spirit.

Suddenly, they had a miraculous ability to speak languages they had never learned. Those who were in Jerusalem for the festival heard the gospel in their own languages and could bring it back home with them, spreading the Christian faith far and wide. As the story continues in the second chapter of the book of Acts, St. Peter was inspired by the Holy Spirit and preached the first official Christian homily. Many people were convinced and convicted by the message and asked what they should do. Peter's answer was "Repent and be baptized," and Luke tells us that about three thousand people joined the Church that day (Acts 2:14–41).

And so the Christian celebration that commemorates this event has been called Pentecost, too, after the Jewish holiday. But again, we should be clear: it's not that the Holy Spirit was absent in the world before this. And it's not that the Holy Spirit hadn't been given to believers before this (see John 20:22). But Pentecost is the moment when the Holy Spirit was given not only to inspire or empower someone for a particular task but also to live within all who commit themselves to Christ, in a way that had not been available to humanity before the Ascension.

The effect this had on the apostles was significant, because the coming of the Holy Spirit is what turned them from the cowards who fled when Jesus was arrested into the bold evangelists who would be willing to give their lives for the gospel. After Jesus' death, they were scattered sheep without their Shepherd. And certainly, their experiences with the risen Lord must have given them some strength, although even then they were still basically laying low, living in hiding. But when the Holy Spirit rested on them as tongues of fire, they took to the streets and told all who would listen about Jesus and their relationship with him.

Where was Mary?

There is no doubt that Mary was there in the upper room with the apostles. In fact, she was the one person there who had been overshadowed by the Holy Spirit before. Some of the apostles had also received the Spirit when Jesus breathed on them after his Resurrection and gave them the authority to absolve sins (Jn 20:22–23). But I wonder if Mary "recognized" the power of the Holy Spirit; when some of those who were there may have been wondering what was going on, was she smiling and nodding?

What does it tell us about Jesus?

One thing Pentecost tells us is that Jesus keeps his word. On more than one occasion, he had promised to send the Holy Spirit, and

Pentecost is when he kept that promise. In John 14:15–31, Jesus referred to the Holy Spirit as the "Advocate" and said that the Spirit would "teach you everything and remind you of all that I told you" (see also John 15:26). This is significant, because Jesus was promising that the Holy Spirit would inspire the apostles (including the ones who wrote the New Testament) to get the message right. We do not have to worry that they missed something, because even though they often got it wrong during their time with Jesus, the Holy Spirit would make sure they got it right when they wrote it down, so that it could be faithfully transmitted through all the generations of the Church.

In fact, Jesus actually called the Holy Spirit "another Advocate," implying that Jesus himself was our first Advocate. The Advocate is like a defense lawyer, working on our behalf, pleading our case before the Judge, and interceding for us. Jesus did that, and now the Holy Spirit does as well. Incidentally, the prayer known as the Salve Regina (Hail, Holy Queen) names Mary as our third Advocate with the Father.

There are many things we can say about the Holy Spirit in the Church. But at this point it's important to see that God wishes to accomplish his will through the agency of those who love him. Jesus could have done everything to accomplish his mission all by himself. Instead, he chose to be born of a woman, raised by an adoptive father, and followed and assisted by a sometimes-bumbling band of disciples; then he left the whole thing in the care of an impetuous guy who denied him three times. The very coming of the Holy Spirit was precisely because Jesus chose not to do it all himself but to bring people in—not only into his kingdom but also into his mission. The presence of the Holy Spirit in the world is for the filling, empowering, and inspiring of all those who would work with God to bring about God's will. Jesus could have done it all himself—could still be doing it all himself—but he wants our buy-in.

Not just our intellectual agreement but also our active cooperation. God's providence allows for the cooperation of the human will with the divine will and grace. Another way to say this is that God calls cowards and asks them to be bold. God doesn't call only the strong; sometimes he calls the weak and gives them strength.

What aspects of this mystery should we imitate?

There are times when we are afraid, and all it seems that we can do is beg God for a miracle. There are times when we are confused and wouldn't even know what to ask for if we prayed. There are times when we have failed so badly that we are ashamed to even come to God in prayer. But St. Paul says, "The Spirit helps us in our weakness; for we do not know how to pray as we ought, but that very Spirit intercedes with sighs too deep for words. And God, who searches the heart, knows what is the mind of the Spirit, because the Spirit intercedes for the saints according to the will of God" (Rom 8:26–27). Pentecost was not only for the apostles. Pentecost was for us, too. We must never be too afraid, too confused, or too ashamed to pray. Even if we don't know what to say, we need just ask for the Holy Spirit to be our Advocate. And we must not forget that Mary is our advocate, too, and that she and the other saints want to pray for us. So if all else fails, we ask for Mary to pray for us, and take it from there. When you don't know what to say to God, pray the Rosary!

MEDITATION

The Holy Spirit turns cowards into evangelists. The Holy Spirit turned a persecutor (Paul) into an apostle, and the one who denied Jesus three times (Peter) into the first pope. The Holy Spirit inspired the writing of the scriptures and guided the Church Fathers as they decided which documents to put in the Bible and how to interpret them.

19

THE ASSUMPTION

The Paradox of the Immaculate Conception

What is the Assumption of Mary?

Read Luke 1:39–56.

The Assumption itself is not recorded in the New Testament. The passage I've asked you to read is Elizabeth's reaction to meeting Mary (pregnant with Jesus) and Mary's song, known as the Magnificat. My point in bringing all this out is that, as beautiful as it is, the story of the birth of Christ is really part of a much larger story. That narrative includes not only the Incarnation of Christ but also the way God had prepared the world for his coming from before the beginning of time. We all know how the birth of the Messiah was promised long before by the Hebrew prophets. But many Christians are not as familiar with the ways in which God prepared for the birth of Jesus in the life of his Mother.

Although not specifically spelled out in the Bible, tradition tells us that Mary's own conception and birth took place under miraculous circumstances. Although both of Mary's parents (Sts. Joachim and Anna) were involved in her conception, like Abraham and Sarah, they were thought to be unable to conceive. It was only with God's intervention that they did conceive a daughter, and it was through the miraculous nature of that conception that God ordained that Mary would be conceived *immaculate*, that is, without original sin. She was spared from the effects of original sin, so that she could be a perfectly pure vessel for the conception of the Son of God. This does not mean that Mary didn't need a savior; it just means that the salvation her Son brought was applied to her even before her birth, in order to prepare her to be the Mother of God.

So although there is some confusion about this among non-Catholics, the Immaculate Conception is not a reference to Jesus' virginal conception, and it does not mean that Mary was conceived of a virgin. What it does mean is that Mary was conceived without original sin, and it prepared her for a life in which she would have no personal sin. By the grace of God, she was to be the only perfectly innocent human after the Fall, other than Jesus himself. She was *full of grace*, or entirely sanctified, from the moment of her conception, and that never diminished throughout her life.

One result of Mary's Immaculate Conception and sinlessness is that she was preserved from the *corruption* of sin. This means, among other things, that her body would never decay. And yet there is no tomb of Mary where you can go to see her body incorrupt. That's because her body is no longer on the earth. After her death, her body was *assumed* into heaven with her soul. And this is what we call her assumption. As I mentioned above, Mary's assumption is her resurrection, because shortly after her death, her body was raised to be reunited with her spirit, and she was welcomed into the heavenly realm whole: both body and spirit.

Assumption, however, is not the same thing as ascension. Jesus ascended, because he was able to ascend himself, under his own power. But Mary is not divine, so she has no divine power of her own to ascend into heaven. She had to be brought up by her Son. Ascension is active. Assumption is passive.

Some Christians believe that Mary never died but experienced something similar to the prophets Enoch and Elijah when they were taken up into heaven without dying. But the ancient teaching of the Church is that Mary did die and there was a funeral. According to early Christian legends, all the apostles were miraculously transported to her bedside from all over the world so that they could say goodbye to her and pay their last respects.

Early Christian depictions of Mary's assumption may seem strange to us now because Mary is not shown floating up to heaven; that might give the impression that she was doing it on her own. Instead, her body is shown lying on a platform, where it would be in preparation for burial. Jesus is there, standing over her body, holding what looks like a baby. That is actually Mary's soul, depicted as a smaller version of Mary. Jesus has returned from heaven with her soul three days after her death, to reunite her soul with her body and bring her into heaven, body and soul.

Where was Mary?

We read in the Gospel of John that Jesus entrusted his Mother to the Beloved Disciple (Jn 19:25–27). Tradition says that Mary went to live with John in Ephesus, where he would become the bishop of Asia Minor. However, the legends that describe the assumption of Mary place her in either Bethlehem or Jerusalem at the time of her death, even though they put John in Ephesus.

Some versions of the story say that she passed only a couple of years after Jesus' Ascension. It seems unlikely that John was in Ephesus that early, especially since Paul was in Ephesus as late as the mid-fifties of the first century and wrote to the Ephesians (without mentioning John) in the early sixties. It's hard to say whether the book of Acts would have mentioned the death and assumption of Mary if it had happened by the time Acts was written. In any case, all the accounts seem to agree that Peter and Paul were still alive when Mary died, which puts her death before the mid-sixties. If she did live into the mid-sixties, she would have been in her eighties.

As the legends tell us (but with conflicting details) the apostles held a funeral for Mary. They were preparing to bury her body, but on the third day after her death, Jesus came bringing her spirit, and she was raised from death. He then brought her, body and spirit, into heaven with him. So there is no tomb of Mary (though some ancient pilgrim itineraries do include a supposed or would-be tomb of Mary in Jerusalem). The only "relics" of Mary are the relics of the Nativity, such as bits of rock from the cave where Jesus was born (held in a reliquary in the church of Santa Croce in Gerusalemme in Rome), and some wood from a manger or crib where the baby Jesus once slept (in the church of Santa Maria Maggiore in Rome).

What does it tell us about Jesus?

Just as Jesus kept his promise to send the Spirit, he will keep his promise to raise us up on the last day. We are assured of this because we can see that he has already done so with his Mother; she is the first to be raised. In fact, one could say that the whole message of scripture, both Old and New Testaments, includes the thread that God is faithful and trustworthy, and keeps his promises. The coming of Jesus was itself a promise kept, and now we put our trust in him and in his promise of resurrection and eternal life. Jesus' incarnation is the very embodiment of God's plan for our salvation, and his promises kept.

God prepared for the coming of Jesus in many ways, one of which was that he worked it out so that his Mother would be the Ark of the New Covenant, without the stain of sin and the consequences of corruption. Her womb was ready to be the pure vessel that would contain the Word the God. The Father, in his omniscient foreknowledge, saw that she would receive her vocation willingly, and would say "yes" (*fiat*) to the Incarnation. So

God proactively intervened in her own conception, so that she would be the Immaculate One, the one who would bring the Son of God into the world.

Finally, we can think of the depiction of Jesus at Mary's assumption as lovingly holding her soul like a baby. It is a beautiful image that parallels all the images we see of Mary holding Jesus as a baby. But the roles are reversed: The Mother who once cradled the Christ child is now cradled by him. The Mother who once protected and carried him is now protected and carried by him into the heavenly realm. And so we can see that Jesus cares for our souls. He wants to protect our souls, and ultimately to bring them—eventually with our bodies—into heaven with him.

What aspects of this mystery should we imitate?

Mary is the living witness and example of humility and obedience leading to blessing. When we follow Mary's example in her *fiat*—her saying "yes" to God's will—we will also follow her in resurrection. When St. Paul says we will be taken up (see 1 Thessalonians 4:16–18; 1 Corinthians 15:51–58), that will be *our* assumption. Mary's assumption is a foreshadowing of the fulfillment of the promise of the "last trumpet," in a similar way as the Eucharist is a foretaste of the heavenly banquet. And just as Mary entrusted her soul to Jesus, we must do the same.

MEDITATION

Mary has been raised, body and soul, into heaven. She is the first one to receive Jesus' promise of resurrection, and we hope to follow.

20.

THE CORONATION OF MARY
The Paradox of the Queen of Heaven

What is the Coronation of Mary?

Read Revelation, chapter 12.

The Coronation, or Crowning, of Mary is her entry into the heavenly realm after her assumption. We speak of this as her coronation because we believe that this is when she takes her rightful place as the Queen of Heaven, the Queen of the Saints, and the Queen Mother of the King of the kingdom.

Chapter 12 in the book of Revelation (like most of that book) is highly symbolic in its language. It leaves room for multiple levels of interpretation, but there are a few things we can say for certain. The woman in John's vision is Mary, the Mother of Jesus. This is clear because she gives birth to the Child who will rule all the nations. John tells us that he saw her crowned with twelve stars—that is, her pedigree is as royalty of the Chosen People. Mary is the last Queen of Israel and the first Christian, because she was the first to say "yes" to Jesus, and to welcome him into his life as her Lord.

As we noted above, this passage in Revelation also includes the part where the Church is called "the rest of her children, those who keep the commandments of God and hold the testimony of Jesus." We are "the rest of her children." From the moment Jesus said to John,

"Behold your Mother," Mary became the Mother of John, and by extension, the Mother of the Church. All Christians are her children.

The demonic spirit that was behind Herod's attempt to kill the infant Jesus was the same demonic spirit that was behind the persecution of the Church in John's day, and is the same demonic spirit that energizes the persecution of the Church in whatever form it takes today. But Mary intercedes for all of her children, from her enthroned position as Queen Mother of Heaven.

Where was Mary?

Mary's assumption puts her in heaven, with her body, which is unlike the other saints. She is the only one there (other than Jesus) who is fully perfected in a reunited spirit and body. In John's vision she is not only crowned with stars; she is clothed with the sun, with the moon under her feet.

In the beautiful mosaics at the two great Marian churches in Rome, Santa Maria Maggiore and Santa Maria in Trastevere, Mary shares a single throne with her Son. At Santa Maria Maggiore, Jesus is placing a crown on her head. This church, the largest basilica dedicated to Mary in the world, was built shortly after the worldwide Church council of Ephesus (the Fourth Ecumenical Council) in the year 431. The mosaic itself was made later, but the church was built, in part, to celebrate the Church's official affirmation of Mary's title "Mother of God." We know that the Church has used this title of Mary at least since the third century, as we can see from the third-century prayer called Sub Tuum Praesidium (in English, "Under Your Protection"). You can find translations of both Greek and Latin versions on the internet, but this is my translation:

> Holy Mother of God, uniquely pure and blessed,
> We take refuge under your compassion.

> Do not ignore our prayers in our time of need,
> But free us from danger. Amen.

This was a prayer for Mary's intercession, originally from the time of persecution of the Church. Mary is Mother of God, Mother of the Church, and the Queen Mother of Heaven. Jesus' elevation of her to a position of sharing the heavenly throne with him speaks to the honor and dignity of women in general: in part for the way they directly cooperate with God in creating life, but more specifically to Mary's role in making the salvation of humanity possible.

What does it tell us about Jesus?

Way back in the fifth century, there was a bishop who tried to get the Church to stop calling Mary "Mother of God" (in Greek, *Theotokos*). He argued that "Mother of God" makes it sound as if you're saying "Mother of the Father," which can't be right. He wanted to change the title to "Mother of Christ." It became such a big controversy that it had to be discussed at a worldwide council of bishops, the Council of Ephesus (AD 431). There was a lot of drama there, which I won't go into, but the consensus of the Church Fathers (and the conclusion of the council) was that it *is* appropriate to call Mary the Mother of God, because she is the Mother of Jesus, who is God. He has both natures, true humanity and true divinity, in his one person, and you can't separate them. If you did, it would sound as if you were saying that the humanity of Jesus was in Mary's womb, but his divinity was not. But that's not right. The whole person of Jesus Christ—humanity and divinity—came into the world through the womb of Mary, and so we may call her the Mother of God.

What does this say about Jesus? It tells us that the Church is, and has always been, adamant about the divinity of Christ. It is non-negotiable. It also tells us that you can't separate Christ's divinity from his humanity, as if "Jesus" is the name for his humanity, and "Christ" is the name for his divinity, or something like that. You can't separate the two natures without making Jesus seem as though he has multiple personalities. So when we call Mary the Mother of God, we are not only saying something significant about Mary but also affirming the divinity of Christ, and the unity of his two natures. We are affirming that God came into the world through a woman, and that he became one of us by taking on a human nature from a woman and uniting it to his divinity so that the two natures would be inseparable. And that is how he would save us: by taking on our nature, redeeming it, and glorifying it. He would save his Mother first, proactively at the moment of her conception, so that she could be the pure vessel through whom he would come into creation to save the rest of us.

What aspects of this mystery should we imitate?

We know that Mary is not divine, but short of making her into a goddess, our respect for her cannot be overstated. When we think of these lofty titles for Mary: Queen of Heaven, Mother of God, Mother of the Church, and so forth, we are expressing our gratitude for Mary's role in our salvation, and for her ongoing intercession for "the rest of her children." But we should always remember that these titles don't just tell us something about Mary; they always also tell us something important about Jesus. And we should always remember that Mary's role in the Church and in salvation history is not to point to herself, but to point to her Son and say, "Do whatever he tells you."

MEDITATION

Mary shares in the rule of her Son and is given the honorary title of Queen of Heaven, but she is not the fourth person of the Trinity. As Mother of God, Mary is the Queen Mother of the heavenly realm, Queen of the Saints.

FINAL THOUGHTS

The Rosary is a "means of grace," or a channel of grace, which means that grace comes to us when we pray the Rosary. Grace is nothing less than God's presence, and God's love, mercy, compassion, and forgiveness in action. It is also God's power to help us be the people God wants us to be in the world. St. Padre Pio used to say that the Rosary is a weapon. It is a weapon against the enemies of the Church, wherever they are found: heresy, schism, persecution, and the distortion of traditional values. St. John Paul II said that the Rosary is also an aid to ecumenism, something that can draw Christians together. This is why I always say that the Rosary is not just for Catholics. The traditional (Dominican) Rosary can be prayed by any Christian who is willing to incorporate the intercession of Mary into his or her devotion, and other versions (chaplets or crowns) can be prayed by those Christians who are not yet ready to ask for Mary's intercession. Therefore, I encourage you to share the Rosary with Catholics and other Christians, and find ways to pray it (or some version of it) together.

Over the years, some Protestants have objected to the Rosary because they have said the repetition of prayers is useless. They often cite Jesus' words to the Pharisees in Matthew 6:7, "In praying, do not babble like the pagans, who think that they will be heard because of their many words." (Some translations of the Bible use phrases such as "vain repetition," but this is not an accurate translation of the Greek text.) When Jesus said this, he was criticizing not the repetition of prayers but "the hypocrites, who love to stand and pray in the synagogues and on street corners so that others may see them." In other words, Jesus was criticizing the "many words" of those who want to be admired by others for their eloquence. And since Jesus himself taught his disciples to repeat the Our Father, he certainly was not criticizing the use and repetition of pre-written prayers.

In fact, the repetition of the prayers is to our benefit, since our human minds tend to wander. By praying a prayer more than once, we will be able to focus on one part when we say it one time, and another part when we say it another time, thereby truly meaning every word by the time we are done. This can actually be a more sincere way to pray than just praying something once, and perhaps only really focusing on part of it, and then moving on. The repetition of the prayers helps us move beyond mere words into meditation, and even into contemplation. Perhaps most importantly, it is one way that God has given us to pray when "we do not know how to pray as we ought," when the Holy Spirit intercedes for us "with inexpressible groanings" (Rom 8:26).

As St. John Paul II said, to pray the Rosary is to learn to see Jesus from Mary's point of view, and to pray to Jesus with Mary. It is, of course, not the worship of Mary but a way to direct our whole hearts and lives *to* Jesus *through* Mary.

Appendix A

HOW TO PRAY THE ROSARY

The Traditional Rosary: A Christ-Centered Rosary

When we talk about the "traditional" Rosary, we are talking about the way the Rosary is most often prayed, but the truth is that there are many ways to pray the Rosary, and many ways to pray using rosary beads. Even with the Rosary as it was promoted by St. Dominic, the way that the prayers are organized has changed over the years. For example, the addition of the Luminous Mysteries by St. John Paul II occurred as recently as 2002. The Rosary has gone through a kind of development, and even now, there is room for regional variations and some measure of personal freedom to modify the form.

There is also some variation (depending on who you ask) about "where" a few of the prayers go on the rosary beads: for example, whether the Glory Be goes on a bead or on the string between beads. This is not a serious concern, and you can do whatever makes sense to you. In any case, here we will highlight the way you are most likely to encounter the praying of the Rosary in parish or group settings.

Remember that the *Rosarium* is a series of prayers, so even when we say we are praying the Rosary, we are talking about the prayers, not specifically the beads themselves. The beads are an aid to prayer, a means to an end (and a beautiful one at that), but they are not an end in themselves. This is not to minimize the way in which a string of rosary beads can be a beautiful work of art, and/

or a precious icon, sometimes even a holy heirloom (if blessed) or contact relic. But the truth is that a person could pray the prayers without the beads and still be praying the Rosary.

Always keep in mind that while we are praying the prayers of the Rosary, we are meditating on key events in the life of Jesus through the eyes of Mary. The prayers below have been distilled from what is contained in the chapters. They give you some suggestions for what to visualize and think about as you pray the prayers, especially the Hail Mary prayers of each decade (series of ten beads).

There are five decades in a Rosary, and there are five mysteries to meditate on in each of the four groups. On Mondays and Saturdays, meditate on the Joyful Mysteries. On Thursdays, meditate on the Luminous Mysteries. On Tuesdays and Fridays, meditate on the Sorrowful Mysteries. On Wednesdays and Sundays, meditate on the Glorious Mysteries. Some people prefer to substitute the Joyful Mysteries on Sundays in Advent and Christmas, and substitute the Sorrowful Mysteries on Sundays in Lent.

When we look at the prayers, there are at least two versions. One version uses archaic, but treasured, language, including older English words such as "thee" and "thou." Another version uses the modern equivalents of these words. Many people prefer to pray using more modern language, but if you pray the Rosary in a group, you will often find the group defaulting back to the older language. I am not advocating for either version of the prayers; in fact I think you should know them both. So I will use the modern words, but put the older words in parentheses. I tend to prefer the more modern version, but you should feel free to pray in the way that feels right for you. So here is the order of the prayer of the traditional Rosary. The prayers themselves follow below.

On the Crucifix: *Make the Sign of the Cross and say the Apostles' Creed.*

On the first single bead: *Pray the Our Father.*

On the series of three beads: *Pray three Hail Mary prayers.*

On the chain (string) or the second single bead: *Pray the Glory Be.*

On each of the five decades (large or offset single bead and series of ten beads):

> On the offset single bead: *Announce the mystery for meditation. Take a moment of silence to visualize the scene in question. Pray the Our Father.*
>
> On the series of ten beads: *Pray ten Hail Mary prayers.*
>
> At the end of the decade: *Pray the Glory Be and then (optional) the Fatima Prayer.*

After completing all five decades, you'll be back at the medal:

Pray the Hail Holy Queen.

Pray the Closing Prayer.

Make the Sign of the Cross.

The Rosary Prayers

SIGN OF THE CROSS

(Pray the words while crossing yourself.)

> In the name of the Father, and of the Son, and of the Holy Spirit. Amen.

APOSTLES' CREED

> I believe in God, the Father almighty, creator of heaven and earth,
> and in Jesus Christ, his only Son, our Lord,
> who was conceived by the Holy Spirit, born of the Virgin Mary,

suffered under Pontius Pilate, was crucified, died, and
was buried;

he descended into hell; on the third day he rose again
from the dead;

he ascended into heaven,

and is seated at the right hand of God the Father
almighty.

He will come again in glory to judge the living and
the dead.

I believe in the Holy Spirit, the holy catholic Church,
the communion of saints,

the forgiveness of sins, the resurrection of the body,
and the life everlasting. Amen.

OUR FATHER (THE LORD'S PRAYER)

Our Father, who art in heaven, hallowed be your (thy)
name.

Your (thy) kingdom come; your (thy) will be done on
earth as it is in heaven.

Give us this day our daily bread

and forgive us our trespasses as we forgive those who
trespass against us.

and lead us not into temptation, but deliver us from
evil. Amen.

HAIL MARY

Hail Mary, full of grace. The Lord is with you (thee).
Blessed are you (art thou) among(st) women
and blessed is the fruit of your (thy) womb, Jesus.
Holy Mary, Mother of God, pray for us sinners
now and at the hour of our death. Amen.

GLORY BE

Glory be to the Father and to the Son and to the Holy Spirit,

as it was in the beginning, is now, and ever shall be, world without end. Amen.

FATIMA PRAYER

O my Jesus, forgive us our sins. Save us from the fires of hell.

Lead all souls into heaven, especially those in most need of your (thy) mercy. Amen.

HAIL, HOLY QUEEN

Hail, Holy Queen, Mother of Mercy, our life, our sweetness, and our hope.

To you (thee) do we cry, poor banished children of Eve.

To you (thee) do we send up our sighs,

mourning and weeping in this valley (vale) of tears.

Turn then, most gracious advocate, your (thine) eyes of mercy toward us,

and after this our exile, show unto us

the blessed fruit of your (thy) womb, Jesus.

O clement, O loving, O sweet Virgin Mary.

Pray for us, O Holy Mother of God,

That we may be made worthy of the promises of Christ. Amen.

CLOSING PRAYER

O God, whose only begotten Son, by his life, Death, and Resurrection,

has purchased for us the rewards of eternal life, grant,
  we beseech you (thee),
that while meditating on (upon) these mysteries of
  the most holy Rosary
of the Blessed Virgin Mary,
we may imitate what they contain and obtain what
  they promise,
through the same Christ Our Lord. Amen.

PRAYABLE MEDITATIONS FOR A CHRIST-CENTERED ROSARY

The Joyful Mysteries (Mondays and Saturdays)

THE ANNUNCIATION: A VIRGIN MOTHER

Lord, you called Mary to be a Virgin Mother, one who remained a virgin as a mother. You made her the Untier of Knots and the Ark of the New Covenant. Lord, you prepared Mary to be your Mother long before you were conceived in her womb. Jesus, prepare us, too, for your presence within us.

THE VISITATION: THE MOTHER OF GOD

Lord, you are eternal and yet you made Mary the Mother of God, the Seat of Wisdom, and the Mother of the Church. She is all these things only because she contained the uncontainable Word of God in her womb by your grace. Jesus, empower us to carry you in our hearts.

THE NATIVITY: THE HELPLESS KING

Lord, you are the Creator who was willing to take the risk to subject yourself to creation. You are the all-powerful One who was willing to limit yourself and become vulnerable. Jesus, you accepted the frailty of the human condition; help us to transcend it by your grace.

THE PRESENTATION: THE HUMBLE GOD

Lord, you are the humble God, the divine human, the all-powerful but self-limiting Savior. Jesus, show us your glory in our limitations, and teach us to embrace obedience and humility.

THE FINDING OF JESUS IN THE TEMPLE: TOUGH LOVE

Lord, your love can be tough love, training us to be more holy. Jesus, show us that your love is always merciful and give us the grace to submit to your guidance so that we, too, may grow in wisdom.

The Sorrowful Mysteries (Tuesdays and Fridays)

THE AGONY IN THE GARDEN: TWO WILLS IN ONE PERSON

Lord, your agony in the garden was the agony of inner conflict. You experienced human weakness and struggled to embrace the Father's will. Jesus, show us the power of perfect obedience and give us the grace to cooperate fully with your will.

THE SCOURGING AT THE PILLAR: IMPASSIBLE SUFFERING

Lord, you came to live a human life and were willing to subject yourself to brutality from the ones you came to save. Though your divinity could not suffer, in your incarnation you submitted to suffering voluntarily, so that we, who could not escape suffering, could know peace. Jesus, help us to find you when we experience suffering or pain.

THE CROWING WITH THORNS: THE SUBJECTED KING

Lord, although you are the highest authority in the universe, you allowed people to belittle and mock you. Through your own complete humiliation, you raised humanity up and out of its debased condition. Give us the grace to use any power or authority we possess in service to others.

THE CARRYING OF THE CROSS: SILENT WISDOM

Lord, you accepted the injustice of false accusations and charges without complaining or protesting, and carried a burden that was not yours. You did this so that we who are guilty could be acquitted of our sins. Jesus, give us the grace to speak out when we should and the wisdom to know when to be silent.

THE CRUCIFIXION: A DYING GOD

Lord, you accepted death willingly so that we, who do not deserve eternal life, could have it anyway. Jesus, help us to lay down our lives and love others even when they do not love us in return.

The Luminous Mysteries (Thursdays)

THE BAPTISM OF JESUS: AN UNNECESSARY NECESSITY

Lord, Baptism was not necessary for you, but it was necessary for us. By stepping into the water, you sanctified it as a sacramental element and made it our gateway to divine life. Give us the grace to see what others need, and the willingness to provide what may seem unnecessary to us.

THE WEDDING AT CANA: THE MUNDANE MADE HOLY

Lord, you make everyday things holy and give us permission to sanctify the rhythm of our lives by punctuating our days, weeks, months, and years with cycles of repentance and celebration. Jesus, help us to recognize the sanctity that is hidden in the mundane.

THE PROCLAMATION OF THE KINGDOM: NOW AND NOT YET

Lord, you taught us that the reality of your kingdom is *both* here now *and* not here yet. It is concealed, and in us, but someday it will be revealed, and we will be in it. Jesus, plant the seed of your kingdom in our hearts and give us the perseverance to tend to your kingdom in the world, knowing that it will not be fully grown until you return.

THE TRANSFIGURATION: HIDDEN GLORY

Lord, you reveal more of yourself to us when we get away from the distractions of the world and find a quiet place to focus on you. Jesus, show us your glory, and teach our hearts to long for the day when we will see you "face-to-face."

THE INSTITUTION OF THE EUCHARIST: SEEING THE INVISIBLE

Lord, you gave us yourself in Holy Eucharist. Your Body and Blood, truly present, cannot be perceived by human senses, but only with the eyes of faith. Jesus, help us to see beyond what is visible and recognize you in the breaking of the bread.

The Glorious Mysteries (Wednesdays and Sundays)

THE RESURRECTION: THE RESURRECTION BODY

Lord, your Resurrection means that death is no threat to us and that those who die in you will also rise with you. Jesus, strengthen in us the hope of redemption and help us to trust that our bodies, like yours, will be raised for eternal life.

THE ASCENSION: GLORIFIED HUMANITY

Lord, you humbled yourself and came down to take on a human nature so that you could raise human nature up to be in union with the divine. Jesus, give us the grace to believe that you will complete your work in us and bring us into the light of your divine glory.

PENTECOST (THE GIFT OF THE HOLY SPIRIT): BOLD COWARDS

Lord, your Holy Spirit turns cowards into evangelists, a persecutor into an apostle, and one who denied you into the first among your shepherds. Jesus, renew the gift of your Holy Spirit in us, take away our fears, and give us the boldness we need to follow you.

THE ASSUMPTION OF MARY: THE IMMACULATE CONCEPTION

Lord, you make promises and keep them. With the assumption, you raised Mary, body and soul, into heaven and made her the first to fully receive your promise of resurrection. Jesus, keep us close to you, and help us to entrust our eternal destiny to your merciful love.

THE CORONATION OF MARY: THE QUEEN OF HEAVEN

Lord, you gave Mary a share in your rule and crowned her the Queen Mother of the heavenly realm. Jesus, lead us always closer to you, and give us the grace of serving you forever in your eternal kingdom.

NOTES

1. If you're interested in reading more on the meaning of the book of Revelation, and how it is a prophetic expansion on Jesus' preaching about the kingdom, I present it in detail in my book *The Wedding of the Lamb*.

2. For more on the resurrection body and its implications, see my book *What Really Happens after We Die (There Will Be Hugs in Heaven)*.

James L. Papandrea is a Catholic author, professor, speaker, and musician. He teaches Church history and historical theology at Garrett-Evangelical Theological Seminary at Northwestern University. Papandrea is a fellow of the St. Paul Center for Biblical Theology and also serves as a consultant for adult faith formation.

After earning his master's degree from Fuller Theological Seminary, Papandrea spent several years focusing full time on youth and music ministries and serving as a consultant in youth ministry. He earned his doctorate in the history and theology of the early Christian church from Northwestern. He has also studied Roman history at the American Academy in Rome.

Papandrea is the author of a number of books for academic and general audiences, including *The Early Church (33–313)*, *A Week in the Life of Rome*, *From Star Wars to Superman*, and *Trinity 101*. He has appeared on EWTN TV and a number of Catholic radio shows. He is a member of the Society of Biblical Literature, the North American Patristics Society, and the Catholic Association of Music. Papandrea lives in the Chicago area.

www.JimPapandrea.com
YouTube: JimPapandrea

AVE

AVE MARIA PRESS

Founded in 1865, Ave Maria Press,
a ministry of the Congregation of
Holy Cross, is a Catholic publishing
company that serves the spiritual and
formative needs of the Church and its
schools, institutions, and ministers;
Christian individuals and families; and
others seeking spiritual nourishment.

For a complete listing of titles from

Ave Maria Press

Sorin Books

Forest of Peace

Christian Classics

visit www.avemariapress.com

AVE MARIA PRESS
Notre Dame, IN
A Ministry of the United States Province of Holy Cross